NATIVE AMERICAN
CREATION STORIES
of
FAMILY and FRIENDSHIP

Addison Moura

NATIVE AMERICAN
CREATION STORIES
of
FAMILY and FRIENDSHIP

Stories Retold
by
Teresa Pijoan

SUNSTONE
PRESS

SANTA FE

Illustrations by Claire Marie Connally.
Cover painting by Nicole Diane Garling.

Sunstone books may be purchased for educational, business, or sales promotional use.
For information please write: Special Markets Department, Sunstone Press,
P.O. Box 2321, Santa Fe, New Mexico 87504-2321.

Book and Cover design ◆ Vicki Ahl
Body typeface ◆ Granjon LT Std
Printed on acid free paper

Library of Congress Cataloging-in-Publication Data

Pijoan, Teresa, 1951-
   Native American creation stories of family and friendship / stories retold by Teresa Pijoan.
      p. cm.
   ISBN 978-0-86534-833-2 (softcover : alk. paper)
   1. Indians of North America--Folklore. 2. Indian mythology. 3. Creation--Mythology.
I. Title.
   E98.F6P53 2011
   299.7'124--dc23
                              2011029710

WWW.SUNSTONEPRESS.COM
SUNSTONE PRESS / POST OFFICE BOX 2321 / SANTA FE, NM 87504-2321 /USA
(505) 988-4418 / ORDERS ONLY (800) 243-5644 / FAX (505) 988-1025

This book is dedicated to

Mrs. Agnes Saiz Sandoval and Robert F. Gallo

Thank you for being dear friends and for patiently helping me over the years with your expertise.

CONTENTS

Foreword

A myth is defined as a traditional or legendary story, usually concerned with deities or demigods. Myths, especially creation myths, contain elements of magic and magical thinking; animals speak, animals become people, people become animals, the dead come back to warn or watch over us. God(s) roam around the dark and bring forth light and all matter of things, leaving us to ask, who created the creator?

Did the people who created these myths really believe them? Yes and no. Only a small child would expect a dog to talk or Grandma to come back and give him a cookie and a hug. However, myths contain truths that can be believed—that the universe is good or bad, that animals are helpful or harmful, that your neighbors are friends or enemies.

Myths are a way to try to make sense out of nonsense. They are also entertainment. Imagine living in a world where the only light at night is a small fire. It's too dark to do most work and too dangerous to move around very much. So people sat around the fire and sang and talked. They gossiped and told stories. Some people are better at telling stories than others. Those people gained status in the group and became the storytellers and sometimes shamans and were called on to talk more often than others. They told stories they had heard and made up new stories. The stories were about the world they lived in. Sometimes the stories asked the "big questions"—where did we come from, where are we going, how did the world get started, what happens when we die? This is how myths are born.

Some of the myths in this book follow the theme of siblings. Sibling rivalry depends on the individuals but also on age differences. Sibs more than three years apart live in such a different world that there is little overt rivalry. Resentment, yes, rivalry no. Resentment of the older that they must look after the younger, "don't hit your little brother," "take her hand when you cross the street." Resentment of the younger that they never get to make any decisions and are always getting hand me downs. Mythic rivalry is often on a whole different level than this and sometimes contains mayhem and murder. But where did Cain and Abel find wives?

Here's a modern creation story. Take a glass flask found in bio and chem labs and put in seawater and add some of the components found in the early Earth atmosphere such as methane, nitrogen, and ammonia. Then zap it with electricity to simulate lightning and seal the flask. Walk away and come back in a couple of weeks and you will find amino acids in the water.

That experiment was first done about fifty years ago. The problem was that the amino acids just sat there. They didn't combine and recombine to become more complex. Recently the experiment was repeated. The researcher tried adding various components, one at a time. When steam, available long ago from volcanoes, was added the amino acids became active and evolved. Once you have viable amino acids it's just a matter of time before you have amoebas, trilobites, sharks, dinosaurs and people.

There is some evidence that pre-literate people handled story memories differently than those of us who rely on the printed page. The Bhagavad Gita, an (East) Indian saga, contains thousands of lines and was created over two thousand years ago. When it was first written down, a couple of centuries ago, from four separate groups of storytellers, in different parts of the country there were only a handful of words (not lines) different in the four versions.

The Bards of Ireland and Scotland each knew hundreds of songs/stories. In Ancient Greece the storytellers could recite the entire Iliad from memory, exactly the same each time.

Today, we know that there is a part of the brain which stores some things differently than the memory of where we put our car keys or when Columbus discovered America.

Myths and stories may be stored in the area of the brain which houses music. That's a different part from where ordinary memories are found. A musician friend once said. "I have hundreds of songs in my head. Both the music and the lyrics are there complete and all I have to do is call them up, storytellers have this same ability."

We know which group of Native Americans and First Americans (the Canadian term) created each of these myths but we don't know anything about the individual storytellers. We also don't know when the myths originated. Were they brought from Asia ten thousand years ago? Probably these, or similar stories, made that journey but we know also that they have changed over the years. We know that because the geography and animals in the myths reflected the American landscape. We also know they have evolved more recently because some of the stories mention horses, sheep, wheat, ovens and woven blankets, all things that were brought here from Europe.

These myths don't tell us much about creation but they tell an enormous amount about the peoples who told and enjoyed them.

—Barbara Blair

Preface

"Creation myths hold the truths of tradition, religion, and the sacred," Sigmund Freud wrote, "The truths contained in religious doctrines are after all so distorted and systematically disguised that the mass of humanity cannot recognize them as truth." Cultures have developed an appreciation of basic belief systems which they refer to as 'religion.' There are the concepts of the Chinese Tao Te Ching that allow the feminine principle of 'yin' to remain free from the male principle of the 'yang,' for the wisdom of the female was honored above all as the 'truth.' Men and women have shared the leading roles in 'belief systems' throughout the Ancient World of the Greek and Roman histories, as well. The pantheon of gods had dominant males, but they had little power against the forceful goddesses who ruled beside them and could deter their wishes. The Christian Bible relates to a time when both woman and man lived together with peace their priority in life. The Eastern Religions hold the power of the male deities as holders of the truth, yet they have equally strong and powerful opposites with the female deities. The balance of the Germinator and the Reproducer maintained awareness in the importance of life born and life lived.

The old stories, the ways of the before time, were true to those who lived that truth. Today, everyone is busy with their New Life. Most people are too busy to remember how we got here, what we need to do to survive, and how to care for this earth with knowledge of the testings of the past. These stories are to remember the past which will help to prepare us, perhaps, for what yet may come.

The symbolic language holds teachings, but without respecting the old ways, many shall never learn. Human beings have lived throughout millenniums, through floods, enduring droughts, appreciating abundance of food, yet every generation has their own trials to overcome, goals to achieve and rewards to receive or lose. These stories are to remind us of how fragile each one of us is as we struggle to survive youth, middle age, and our older years. It is important to listen and remember for once the truth is gone; we shall certainly be on our own.

The stories included in this book hold the conflicts and compliments of family and/or situations of testing in relationships. Native cultures have lessons to be learned here, just as every culture does. These stories are not unique, yet they may help educate many of us today in finding solutions to similar problems.

Thank you, to my supporters and research assistants: Barbara Blair, Marianne & Neil Hamilton, Alice Lawson, Michael Montoya M.D., Millie DeFabio, Frank Chinisci, Tommy Roe, David Magnus, Reinaldo Garcia, Annie Montoya, Jessica Hash, Arun & Usha Prabhune, Andrea Westforland, Esther Shir, Leann Weller, Miriam Gustafson, Nicole & Joseph Garling, Claire & Lillian Mae Connally, Barbara Pijoan, and my special buddy of all time, Thomas E. Van Etten.

Special thanks to the following who shall speak out and be heard: Rhianon Baca, Casey Beaty, Denise Black, Jazmine Cresap, Adriana del Campo, Virginia Forbes, Monica Garcia, Nathan Garcia, Melody Glass, Patrick Beasley, Daniel Herrera, Andrea Speed, Aaron Sieben, Maria Dlinn, Sandra Lease, Nicole Vigil DVM, Jonathan Milarch, Daniel Murray, Nicholas Otero, Regina Pena, Marquez Richards, Roxanne Sanchez, Katie Seals, Andrea Torrez, Sir Patrick Trujillo, Jesse Wells, Lance White, and the honorable Joshua Woods who holds great bravery and knowledge.

Thank you, Sunstone Press, Jim and Carl for all of your help!

Life is good with these fine people in it; they hold great stories and excellent deeds.

Thank you, one and all.

—Teresa Pijoan

You are pure
      You are good
            You are whole
                  You are as you should be.
                        May the wisdom of the past keep you strong.

Old Tanoan Poem.

Ocean Grandmother / Paiute

The South Valley Library filled with visitors as the snow continued to fall outside. There were four of us at the computers. We were working quickly for there was a line of people waiting to use them. As I printed up my last copy of information a voice spoke up behind me. "Here, these are yours. Are you interested in the reservations further northwest?"

Evidently he had picked up all the papers from the printer thinking they were his. His face glowed with a smile. "If you want to know about the Paiute I can tell you plenty! My family lived through the Great Move and the government's lack of care on the rez."

Running through the falling snow, we crossed the street to a newly opened restaurant. Steaming hot tea fogged up his glasses as he studied my papers. "Some of this is right on the money, but this is way off. You know some people think we are related to the Navaho because we live close to them, but we're not. When I went to the University of New Mexico there were anthro professors there who thought the Paiute were part of the Shoshone Tribe. That's when I quit school. If you don't go out and talk to the people, how are you supposed to know anything? What is written in books comes from other books and what was in those books is not necessarily correct or even close to being right." His tea cup was pushed over to the side of the table.

"There are stories and then there are stories. Knowing the right story is what keeps you on your path. If you don't know what you're talking about because you believed someone else who was misinformed, then you don't know dip. Know what I mean?"

The Storyteller frowned as he told of his people's history, "The 1850s and 1860s were a time when the people were brought under control. Before this, we wandered to California to visit and hunt. Other times, we would go out searching for food or willows for the baskets all the way to the Great Lakes. The land belonged to no one and the people were careful not to upset the land, yet were given the freedom to travel anywhere. We were the caretakers of the land and the animals. There were no boundaries.

"Eighteen forty-eight brought the gold miners. White people went west in droves anyway they could. They traveled usually on the Jedediah Smith route which went from Salt Lake City to Los Angeles. The pioneers and travelers knew the stories about the wild Indians and came prepared. Many Paiute Indians were killed standing in their fields. Killing an Indian was fair game.

"The Paiute tried to stay out of harm's way, but people were coming over the hills, through the fields, forests, and everywhere. The Paiute were famous for not killing people, but for stealing their cattle. The cattle were a luxury to them. The cattle were herded across their lands, their homes, and once they were on their lands, they were thought to be property of the Paiute family.

"The Paiute were stricken with disease. This was believed to have been brought in by the outsiders as Bad Medicine to get rid of the Paiute. Once the disease had passed and there were still some living, the Mormon people moved into the area. They gave some protection from the Gold Miners, but they went after the Paiute spirit, not their land. The Mormons brought the mumps. Thousands of Paiute people died. There were too many dead to have ceremony. The stories of this time are frightening. There was terror everywhere and fear. Many died of choice for all their family was dead from the Mormon curse.

"The Department of the Interior created an office to control land related disputes regarding Indian Affairs in eighteen forty-nine. The gold miners were taking away the traditional lands of many of the Paiute. Then when the Mormons came, they tried to barter land from the Paiute. Later the Indian Claims Commission was created by an act of Congress in nineteen forty-six to rule on claims brought by Indians against the United States and related to the United States government's failure to pay the Indians money due to them for land ownership. The United States government had promised money to the Paiute in exchange for land, but the money never arrived. The Indian Reorganization Act in nineteen thirty-four stopped the policy of allotting plots of land to individuals and encouraged the development of reservation communities. The act also provided for the creation of autonomous tribal governments. Now, individuals could not keep their traditional lands within the family. The land belonged to the whole group and was divided up by the government's agents."

He pushed back his long black bangs. "We have been done wrong by the government in many ways, but one thing they could never do was put us on a reservation far from our home. Our neighbors the Navaho were pushed around all over the place only to end up where they started. We got along just enough to keep at least some of our land. This was good, but we were left with little respect. That hurts."

The large hot apple pie piece was set in front of him. The vanilla ice cream was quickly melting to cover the plate. It only took him a few minutes to eat it up and then he was ready for his telling of Paiute Creation.

[This story was verified with Robert J. Franklin's and Pamela A. Bunte's published story in The Paiute.]

The Story of Ocean Grandmother

*T*here were only animals, land, oceans, and earth. Earth was filled with plants that could talk to all things and all things could talk with the plants. Life was good, aside from each individual personality. Wolf was the Wise Grandfather who lived with his brother Coyote. Coyote was lazy, lazy, lazy. Coyote thought he could get away with anything and no one would notice. Coyote told his wife he was out hunting when he was really out sleeping in a field of sweet grass. Coyote would sleep in his moccasins and then on the way home he would slap them against a hard rock to make them appear worn out from running.

One morning, as Sun was just arriving, there grew on the horizon a blue haze. The plants bent down as the blue haze passed over them. A soft scent of salt floated around in this blue haze which slowly took shape as the sun grew brighter. It was Ocean Grandmother. Rarely did Ocean Grandmother leave her home. Sometimes she delivered sacred messages to animals, birds, or fresh water creatures. Her devotion to the sacred was admired and she was always held in great respect.

Ocean Grandmother of the West moved east across the land.

Heavy was the load hanging from her back which she held over her shoulder by a thick leather strap. The weight did not stop her. She was a determined spirit, a strong spirit, regardless of her ancient age she would make it to her destination.

At the edge of a deep arroyo, Ocean Grandmother stopped. Leaning to the left, she gingerly placed the heavy leather sack down on the dry caliche earth. A thin spider web cloth was removed from her pocket apron. Frail soft blue fingers wiped the dust from her face and then returned the spider web cloth to her apron pocket. Regaining her composure, she called out, "Wolf, Wolf, I have brought you something sacred and you must take it west to Rabbit."

Wolf who was down in his den working on sacred things, turned his head. "Coyote, did you hear something?" Coyote scratched his nose with his hind paw. "No, but it smells like sea salt in here all of a sudden."

Wrinkling up his nose, Wolf sniffed the air. "Ahh, it is Ocean Grandmother. Her voice is as soft as the wind. We best go up and find out what she wants. This is a great honor."

Coyote shook his head. His left ear was inside out and it wouldn't flop down. Wolf led the way, while Coyote continued to shake his head as he walked into the side walls. Wolf waited for him near the entrance. "Coyote, stop shaking! Ocean Grandmother is the grandmother of all life. You want to show her respect, not act stupid. Come here, let me fix that ear." Wolf smacked Coyote along the side of his head and the left ear fell into place. "There, now don't embarrass me."

The two stepped out into the bright sunlight. At first all they could see was a tall blue cloud floating at the edge of the arroyo. Wolf loped up to greet her. "Ocean Grandmother, welcome to our home. How may we help you?"

Ocean Grandmother coughed and then leaned forward to stroke Wolf's ears. Wolf quickly called back to Coyote, "Brother, get Grandmother some water. She is parched from her journey."

Coyote turned quickly to go back into the den for a jug of water. Instead of the den's door he hit the arroyo wall and fell down with a howl. Wolf shook his head. "Take no mind, he will bring water. Please sit and tell me of your visit."

Ocean Grandmother spoke with Wolf in her soft voice. Coyote finally brought the water jug. Ocean Grandmother most politely thanked Coyote who promptly fell down on the ground and rolled over for a tummy rub. Wolf smacked him on the nose with his front right paw. "Get up, you have an important chore to do which will change all of creation."

Coyote quickly got up, shaking the dirt off of his back, and then sat.

"What am I to do, brother?"

Wolf shook his head. "Coyote, this is an important spirit. This sack needs to be taken to Rabbit. Rabbit will know what to do with this. It is a great honor to carry this sack and certainly you are an honorable coyote."

Coyote smiled. "Yes, I can take this important sack to Rabbit. Tomorrow will be a good day to take this sack."

Ocean Grandmother shook her head. "No, this sack must be taken to him immediately. You must do this today or we will all be punished."

Coyote was not one to be scolded or punished. "Yes, Grandmother, I will be on my way."

Wolf pulled Coyote to the side. "Do not open this leather sack." Wolf bared his sharp white teeth and growled, "If you open this sack before you give it to Rabbit, I will rip you apart piece by piece and there will nothing left of you or of your family. Do you understand?" Coyote took the sack from Ocean Grandmother and started on his journey to Rabbit. Coyote threw the sack across his back and loped off to the east. The contents of the bag moved, sometimes kicked him in the ribs, other times they shifted from side to side in the bag. Finally Coyote stopped and dropped the bag. A strange sound came out it. "This must be filled with rattlesnakes! What if Wolf wants to get rid of me? Yes, he wants the snakes to bite me!"

Coyote quickly kicked the bag then ran and hid behind some bushes. He peered out watching it. The contents were squirming, moving. Coyote decided he would quietly open the bag and run for his life. Slowly, he crept up to the bag on his stomach. His teeth pulled at the leather tie ever so silently. His right paw pushed the bag on its side. As it opened he ran for cover. Frightening, white, groping long extensions reached out of the bag. Shapes he had never seen before began to crawl out on all fours. They had no hair, no big ears, no tails. They were terrifying.

Wind blew, tossing dirt and dust everywhere. Wind called out to Coyote, "Grab the bag! Grab the bag! It is not time for these to come out of the bag! Quickly! Grab the bag!" Coyote shivered. Wind did not stop yelling at him. He realized this was very great magic, but only after some of the creatures had run away. Coyote gathered up what small amount of courage he had inside of himself and dashed to the bag. He pulled the leather tie shut with one fast tug and sat down on the opening.

Screams mixed with jutting motions came out of the bag. Coyote listened for Wind. Wind had gone. Slowly, Coyote picked up the bag. Holding it in front of him carefully, he ran west to find Rabbit.

The sun grew hot overhead and beat down on Coyote. Coyote began to feel cursed by this heavy bag. "If I let some more of these creatures out, the bag will be lighter!" Coyote placed the bag near an arroyo. Gently he pulled the leather tie open. Sitting stock still he watched as some of the creatures ran from the bag. Wind blew at him again. "Close the bag, Coyote! Close the bag! You will be destroyed! Close the bag!" Fearing for his life, Coyote pulled on the leather tie and the bag shut. By now he was used to the screaming and banging. Hugging the lighter bag made running easier. As Coyote loped to the horizon he heard someone calling his name. Rabbit came into view.

"Coyote, you were to bring the bag full. What have you done?"

"Rabbit, there were snakes and horrible animals in this bag. I had to let them go or they would have killed me!"

"Coyote, there were no snakes. There is nothing in that bag that would hurt you. You are lazy, a coward, and now you have done permanent damage. The Creator watched you. He told me of your doings!"

Coyote cringed, looking up into the great and powerful Sky. "I wasn't trying to hurt anything."

Rabbit took the bag to the center of the earth. This is near the Colorado River on the north side of the Grand Canyon. Wild deer, berries, pinion nuts, squirrels, and tall trees were in abundance. Rabbit opened the sack. Rabbit chanted to the First People. He soothed their fears. He taught them of survival and of the great spirits who would watch over them. The people stayed. These are the Paiute People. The People who live in the center place of harmony.

Twin Brothers of Life / Iroquois

The New Mexico, July sky was an endless pool of chalk blue. Ducks, heron, and black starlings floated about in the newly irrigated pasture. The two orange tabby cats walked the fence, trying to figure out a way to get to them without getting wet. The African Pygmy goats behind me stood on their high platform, well out of water's way. Every now and then one of them would stamp his hoof to chase away the barn flies. Cisco, my super pup, ran by my side as I moved the hose from one side of the vegetable garden to the other. The snap peas had been excellent and soon it would be time for butter squash and zucchini.

Standing outside the barn, I watched a battered gray pickup with a shell camper turn off the dirt road onto our driveway. The truck bounced over each deep rut with creaks and groans. As it came to a stop, the back of the camper shell opened to release six young women. They jumped down, promptly shook out their long hair, and started taking off their blouses.

A tall lanky man with a beat up cowboy hat stepped out of the driver's side of the gray truck. He looked over the farm, spotted me to call out a "hello!" I waved back to him, meeting him at the front wooden gate. Pushing his old hat back onto his head, he said, "Hey-yah, the storyteller has arrived."

"Yes, I can see that and you brought your audience with you?"

He waved his hand in the air. "Oh, those are my daughters. You said you wanted a story about siblings, well, I have daughters. Six of them are right there. All of them want to wash their hair."

I couldn't help but smile. "Good thing it's July or there would be a problem!" He laughed with me. The young women appeared to be between the ages of nineteen and twenty-four years of age. Quickly, I tried to do the math in my head. Six young women with only six years possibly between them, fast pregnancies.

The young women were pulling out three foot tall water containers that had spigots on the sides. Two of the young women were on top of the camper shell lifting them up, sitting them on the roof of the camper. The others, below them, had disrobed to sparkling white camisole tops over their colorful broom skirts. All of the young women were barefoot. "Quite a sight, isn't it?" He shook out his battered cowboy hat. "Say, you wouldn't mind if I borrowed your facilities for a pit stop, would you?"

"No, no, go ahead. Right through the front door, take your first left and it's at the end of the hall. Help yourself." I pointed to the front door with my right hand and held my dog with the other. "I'll just go and put the dog in the barnyard so he won't jump all over the girls." The storyteller scratched his stubbly face. He first went to the truck and pulled out a small bag, and then he went into the house. I pulled the dog into the barnyard, closed the gate, and fed the critters. It was early, only three o'clock, but somehow I knew this was going to be a busy afternoon.

The young women were busy working with bowls on the tailgate of the truck. I walked over to introduce myself, hoping to get a look at their work. One young woman was grating yucca root with a cheese grater into a yellow porcelain bowl. The young woman next to her was smashing the gratings into another bowl with a big wooden spoon, while her sister was slowly pouring water into the mush. This concoction started to bubble. The younger woman beside them took the bubbly mush and poured it on one of the other sister's wet hair.

This worked up into a fine lather while one of the sisters, on top of the camper shell, was releasing water from the containers down onto her head. Each young woman took turns, each one was soaking wet by the end of this ordeal, all orchestrated with perfect timing. Finally, the towels were pulled out of the back of the camper and the young women started rubbing down each other's long hair.

There were two sisters that did not appear to fit into the group. They were older than the others, had blonde hair down to their knees, and were covered with freckles. When they told me their names were Bridget and Meagan, I had to laugh. "The Celts have taken over the Southwest!" They stared at me.

While they were busy with their hair drying, and shaking out their wet camisoles, I went into the house to cook some dinner. Walking into the house, the smell of men's cologne wafted through the air. There at the end of the hall, with the bathroom door wide open stood the storyteller. He had his back to me and was buck naked, except for his boots and his hat. His hat was dripping water onto his wet boots. Carefully he was ringing out his shirt over the bathtub and then he hung it on the shower rod. As he slowly turned, I hurried into the kitchen.

The house soon filled with the smells of my reheated tamales, freshly cooked fry bread, and vegetarian stew. Slowly, women found their way into the kitchen to help with the setting of the table. One of them ran to the truck, bringing back homemade apple cider and some paper cups. The large dining room table was pulled out to fill almost the whole of the kitchen. Everything was ready. Meagan went in search of her father. The storyteller arrived in his one piece, Johnny drop, long johns. He had on his socks and no hat. Meagan followed him, holding his wet boots and dripping hat. "Can I hang this up outside? Or is there a place I can put these?" I showed her where the clothes line was. She smiled. "Dad forgets to take his clothes off when he takes a shower. I'll just hang his other duds up here until they dry."

Half-way through dinner, my oldest daughter came home from work. She called out as she walked through the front door. I ran to meet her. Her eyes were large when I hugged her. "Mom, what is going on here? Looks like the gypsies have arrived."

"Nicole, don't say a word. The storyteller is here and he brought all his daughters with him. Just put your things down and come to dinner." Nicole laughed at me. "Oh, boy, a storyteller who travels around making stories as he tells them. I love it!"

After everyone had finished eating, the daughters all worked together to clear the table and wash the dishes. The storyteller nodded to the back door. "Mind if we go outside? Tamales have a way of affecting my stomach."

"Yes, we can go outside, it has cooled off. The weather is lovely." I lead him to the back picnic table where we sat down and watched the clouds.

"All right, I guess you have earned your story." He nodded toward the kitchen window. I looked up to see all the daughters laughing and working together.

"Yes, it has been great being with all of you, didn't feel like work at all."

"Well, it's time for a story. The sun is about ready to rest. This story is an old story, all my daughters know this story so to tell it in front of them would make them tired. My great-grandfather wrote this story down and he passed it to my grandfather who passed it to my father and now I hold the story. When the story is finished, I can show you the old notebook. But right now, I think you should hear the story."

I agreed with him. Then he held up his hand. "Just one question. Why are you interested in stories about children and the trials they have with their parents?"

"That's a fair question. I have two daughters and they are difficult. Sometimes they are friends with each other and other times they want to kill each other. As a parent, I can't understand how they compete for love. Each one gets a different kind of love and care, they aren't the same. Perhaps if I hear enough stories, maybe I can figure out how to be a better mother." I pushed the bangs off my forehead.

He laughed hardily. "A better parent! Hah! What a hoot!" He slapped his leg. "Parents are stuck with what they get! I care about my daughters, but found it easier to have as many as possible. That way they are busy with each other! Hah!"

His face became serious. "All right, you feel vulnerable around your daughters. When kids are very small they learn how parents work. Children are professional manipulators. They can read people in a heartbeat to know exactly how to get what they want." Swallowing hard, he stopped long enough to shake his head. "This story should help you realize that children don't need parents to survive, just acceptance. Sometimes they don't even need that, just the belief that they are good people and they can survive. Here is the story, sit back, relax. We have to leave soon for I promised their grandmother I would have them at her house by dawn. She lives in Amarillo, Texas."

As if on cue, all the daughters, including my Nicole, came quietly out to sit beside us. We listened to the story unfold on this lovely summer afternoon.

The Story of Twin Brothers of Life

In the beginning time, there were the Sky People who lived only high above the waters of life. The Sky People lived in great long lodges. The men slept on one side of the great lodge while the women slept on the other. The women placed finely woven mats on the floor of the men's side of the lodge. The women kept their place as was the custom of the Sky people. They did not mingle with the men.

Early in the morning, the men would go hunt and return before sun dusk. The women would tend to the needs of the lodges, such as sweeping, cleaning, skinning animals, and drying jerky. All went well for a time.

There were two, a man and a woman, who were admired, and looked upon with respect who grew to like one another. This was not usual, for there were no children in the Sky Place. People lived, worked, and continued in a manner which was considered completely spiritual. One morning, the woman arose earlier and walked to the men's side of the lodge. She saw the man whom she admired. She went up to him with a branch and began to comb his hair. The man allowed her to comb his hair, for her hands were soft and gentle. When she had finished, she nodded at him and went back to her side of the lodge.

Sometime after this, the man called for his mother to be brought to him. The mother hurried to the men's side of the lodge, for this was most unusual. There she found her son lying on his mat, weak, pale, and barely able to speak or move.

"My son, what has happened to you?" Her son shook his head wearily. "I am going to die. You must hold my head in your hands, look into my face as my life leaves me, and let no one else come near me."

"My son, what do you mean you are going to die? No one leaves this place, no one has died before this?" The mother stroked her son's hair away from his pale face. "Tell me, son, what is it that you have? Are you ill? Have you been hurt?"

Her son steadily studied her eyes. "No, I am going to die. You must hold my head in your hands when you feel my life leaving me, you must look directly into my eyes so that your face is the last face that I see. You must build for me a wooden bed to lie in once my spirit has left me. Do you understand, Mother, do you understand what I am saying?"

His mother shook her head. "No! You cannot die, we are the Sky People. You cannot die!"

"Mother, you must do as I ask. You need to help me. Do as I ask. Once you have made a wooden bed for my body, you must take it up on the mountain over the village of the Sky People. Leave it open, leave it there in the trees on the mountain. Put me on this wooden bed with my beaded wrist guard, my bow and arrows, put my moccasins on my feet, and leave me food and water near by. Mother, you must do this." Silently his breath left his body.

His mother leaned close to him, holding his head in her hands she watched his eyes glaze over and fade. She started to cry. The Sky People, who were outside and unaware of what was happening, all began to cry. They stopped and watched each other, they had no idea why there were tears falling from their eyes. The mother held her son's head until he was no longer warm. She put her hands over his eyes, but they would not close. Quietly, she went outside to get the men to build her son a wooden bed carry.

The son's body was carried up into the mountains.

His beaded leather guard was on his wrist, his moccasins were on his feet, the carefully beaded chest plate was nicely laid out and tied around his chest. Food and water bowls were put all around his wooden bed carry. The Sky People left him there, alone.

The woman from the woman's side of the lodge was saddened to learn of the man's death. None had died in the Sky Place and no one was sure how to behave. But each day, after his death, the woman grew in size. It became difficult for her to walk, to lean over, or to carry a load of wood. She questioned her mother about her condition, but her mother did not know what was wrong with her. Finally, at the time of the high moon in the Sky Place, this woman knelt down outside of the village and gave birth to a fat, healthy, little girl baby. The cries of the infant awoke the village. People from the lodge came running. Some had spears, other bows and arrows, women hovered back afraid of the small screaming baby.

The woman's mother came forward with a blanket. "Here, the little one is cold and frightened, cover her and bring her with you home." They took the baby into the women's lodge. The baby girl grew quickly. At first the Sky People were frightened of the infant, then the toddler who was always running about, getting in their way. At the time of the next high moon, the little girl was almost fully grown. She had long hair down to the back of her knees, she spoke well, and was being taught women's ways.

After the high moon time, the girl began to cry. She cried and cried endlessly. No one knew why she was so upset. Her grandmother came to her mother, asking if the girl had been on the mountain. The mother said, no. Her daughter hadn't left the village, everyone knew where she was for she was always laughing and running.

The mother of the dead son came to the see the girl. "You are so much like my son. You have his eyes. You laugh like him. Would you like to see the place where my son remains on the mountain?" The girl wiped her eyes and, studying the older woman, she said, "Yes, I would like to see this place, can you take me there?" The woman shook her head. "No, I cannot leave the village, but I can tell you where this place is and you can go by yourself." The woman picked up a stick and drew the map of how to go up the mountain to her son's resting place.

The girl left immediately without telling her mother or her grandmother. The trees were thick on the mountain, the birds appeared to be guiding her along with their songs as she ran up the path. Sparkling brooks glowed as she ran by them on her way to the resting place. The young woman was very calm when she saw the man's body. She sat nearby and told him stories of the people in the village. After a time, she returned to the village and told her mother about her visit. Her mother was shocked, but knew better than to scold her child for she felt this was all great magic.

Day-after-day, the daughter went up the mountain. She appeared to be much more at peace when she returned. Life was back to normal, until one time she came down the mountain with the beaded leather wrist guard. She wore it on her thin arm as if it were a trophy. She showed it to all the people. Her mother wanted to take it away from her, but did nothing.

An elder came to the girl and asked, "What possessed you to take the beaded wrist band from the dead man?"

The child glared at him. "I did not take it! My father gave it to me. He told me to keep it, saying that he was my father and this was his gift to me."

The elder shook his head in despair. Day-after-day, she went up onto the mountain and life continued. Then one day she returned with his beaded chest plate.

She walked proudly into the village with it hanging from her neck to her knees. "Look what my father gave me! Isn't it beautiful? He said that I am now fully grown and must go out of the village to meet the man who shall take care of me. It is time for me to leave!" She proudly showed everyone the breast plate.

When she got to the lodge, she asked her mother to make bread for her and to place it in a basket that she had made. Her mother was very unsure of this, but not knowing what else to do, she put the bread in the basket. The men were now asleep on their side of the lodge and the women, aside from her mother and herself, were asleep on the other side of the lodge. The girl took the basket and climbed up the mountain. When she arrived at her father's body, she told him she was ready.

The spirit of the dead father spoke to her, "When it is rising time, you must walk away from the mountain, toward the open land, away from the village. You will spend one night there in the trees. When the sun rises a man will come to you. He will become one with you in spirit. His name is He-Holds-the-Earth. Do not be frightened of him. Now you must rest. When you rise in the morning, there will be a robe for you to wear. Do not be frightened for I will be with you on your journey."

The girl did as she was told. When the sun rose, she dressed in the fine robe, picked up her basket and set out on her adventure. As she walked along the path, she met many strange creatures that were walking toward her. She did not look them in the eye nor did she speak with them. She stayed steady on her path. Finally, she came to a river. A large log came floating down the river and stuck to the side of the bank. The other side of it swung around, hitting the opposite side of the bank. The girl felt her body changing into that of a young woman as she carefully hurried across the log. Once she was on the other side, the log floated gracefully down stream. She walked on a way until she came to a small lodge.

The lodge glowed with bright lights shooting out of the cracks. She stopped to put down her basket filled with bread. She took the mat from under her arm, rolled it out under the trees, and lay down to sleep. The next morning, a man came out of the lodge. He glowed with bright lights all around him. He motioned for her to come into the lodge. She rolled up her mat, picked up her basket and followed him into the lodge of lights. There she put her mat down sideways just below the man's mat. He took her basket from her and tasted the bread. That night he slept on the big mat and she slept on the mat which was near his feet.

She arose in the morning to do her womanly duties. The man came around from the back of the lodge, He handed her a braid of dried corn. "You must soak this and make mush." She placed the corn kernels into the boiling pot until the water was almost gone, and then she went back into the lodge of lights to return with a flat grinding rock and a round hand rock. She carefully lifted the corn out of the hot pot with some green branches and began to grind it down to mush. Once the corn was completely pulverized on the grinding rock, she filled the mud basket pot back up with water and boiled it again.

As she boiled the mush, allowing the water to come to a full boil, the man came to her again.

He spoke firmly to her, "Take off your clothes. You must take off your robe now, fold it beside you, and stand by the boiling pot." She did as she was told.

The pot sputtered, boiling mush leapt up to burn her body. It stuck to her skin. She did not jump back, nor did she cry out for she wanted the man to know how strong she was. Finally, she motioned to him, "Your mush is cooked, it is done." She watched him lift the hot muddied basket off the fire as he poured it into a flat piece of bark. He sat down cross legged and started eating the mush. When he was finished, he clapped his hands. Two dogs appeared from the forest.

He pushed the dogs over to her naked body. The dogs started to lick her where the mush had scorched her skin and stuck. The more they licked the more tender her body became and soon the marks were bleeding. She was brave and strong and did not cry out to him. When the dogs had finished licking off the burned mush, he told them to return to the forest. "You," he said to her, "put your robe back on your body. You will heal quickly, come let us eat this bread that your mother baked for us. For now I will be your man and you will be my woman."

The second day, she was asked to repeat what she had done the previous day. In the afternoon, the man went out hunting and brought back food. That night he ordered her to sleep at his feet and not to stir. The lights in the lodge were bright and the man explained to her that the large tree next to his lodge was called Tooth. The lodge held the light for all of life and the Tooth was the origin of light. She stayed with him for four days.

The following morning, the man told her to return to her village. She picked up her basket, which magically refilled with bread every morning. The strap of the basket was placed firmly on her forehead and her moccasins lead her to the river. A maple log floated down the stream and stuck to the bank of the river. Balancing on it, she hopped to the other side just as she had done before. There were strange men who spoke to her, but she knew these were the Aurora Borealis that wanted to trick her. She ignored them and continued walking. Finally she made it home to her mother.

The people gathered around her to hear her story of adventure, but all she told them was that they needed to remove the roofs of the lodges for food would be coming to them, lots of corn, meat, and squash. It would fall from the sky above and rain down on the lodge. Once the lodges were filled to capacity, the people were to quickly put on the roofs.

The young woman did not stay with the Sky People. She walked up the path to her father's place. That night as the people slept out in the open, there came a great rain. The sky filled with strange dark clouds that dropped huge quantities of food. Com, dried jerky, squash, and fowl flying and squawking in all directions fell from the night sky. After all was quiet, the people hurriedly put the roofs back on the lodges for the young woman was nowhere to be found, but the people knew she was with her father.

The next day the young woman again picked up her basket of bread to be with her man near the tree of Tooth. She traveled all day as before and got there in time to prepare him his dinner. They continued to live a peaceful life. She slept at his feet and he went hunting during the day. It came about that she started to become very uncomfortable. She was quick to answer her man and he noticed that she was growing in size. As she grew in size, he felt weaker and weaker.

He confronted her one day, "Woman, what is going on with you? Why are you so angry with me and what is happening that I am becoming ill?" She stared at him. He did look puny. "I don't know, I'm not happy that is certain. I'm not happy at all. I can't eat, my legs hurt, my back hurts, and I'm tired of living every day the same. This must be your fault. I'm not happy, not at all."

He walked around her. "You're with child, aren't you?"

She snapped back at him, "How can I be with child? We haven't shared a mat, you sleep up there and I sleep at your feet. What are you talking about?" She whirled around to face him. "You're always so careful all the time not to upset anything and yet you don't mind accusing me of something I didn't do. I'm not happy here, not at all and somehow this is all because of you!"

He jumped back from her. She was viciously attacking him. He felt weak and promptly sat down on the ground. "Call the people, you must call the people, for I fear that I am going to die." She glared at him. "I will call the people, but you better not die!"

She sent out word that the people of his forest needed to speak to him. They arrived early the next morning. He-Holds-the-Earth asked some of the men to carry him outside. The people were stunned to see him look so ill. "My people you must help me gain back my strength. You must pull up the Tree called Tooth, place me near the hole with my head on the lap of my woman. You must do this right away, or I will die."

The people went right to work. They sharpened long branches and used these to scoop out the dirt around the Tree of Tooth. They dug and dug all day. Just as the day was ending, one of the men pushed on the tree and it fell down, down, down, down, through a hole to the waters of life below. The people brought her gifts of bread, corn, and jerky. She pushed these under her garment against her large stomach. Quickly, they picked up He-Holds-the-Earth and placed him beside her. Just as she bent over to peer down into the hole, he reached up and pushed her neck. She fell with nothing to hold onto. There was nowhere for her to go but down into the dark waters below.

He-Holds-the-Earth sat up fully recovered. His people pulled him away from the hole. The man made a quick recovery for now he was single again which was the way of the Sky People. It was not their way to be in union with a woman. It was not their way for women to become pregnant. The Aurora Borealis was pleased that the woman with child was no longer living in the sky. Now the life of the Sky People could be normal.

The falling woman stopped being fearful for it did her no purpose. She stared down below to see a blue light. Looking up at her were loons, ducks, and grandfather turtle. Birds flew down and told them that a woman was falling from a hole in the sky and she was coming quickly. They knew of things falling, for a tree had fallen from the sky not long ago and had almost killed some of them. Grandfather Turtle asked the birds to dive down into the waters of life to bring back mud. They tried. Many died, but finally a red eyed duck crawled up onto the back of Grandfather Turtle and dropped mud on his shell. Then she fell into the water and died. Muskrats climbed on the shell of the Grandfather Turtle and began to spread mud all over. The mud multiplied. Soon the carapace became the earth with dirt, mud, and slime growing on his shell everywhere.

The falling woman was getting closer. Her speed had increased. She was a large woman and the birds were frightened she would break Grandfather Turtle's back. The birds all joined together, wing-to-wing to catch her. She fell into their soft feathers and slowed. They gently lowered her onto the back of the Grandfather Turtle.

When she awoke in the morning, she saw that the wood had been used to build a fire. The dried jerky was now a dead deer and the bundle of corn kernels was growing fields of corn plants. She was pleased. She spent the following days building a thatched lodge. Soon she gave birth to a baby girl who was a whirlwind of trouble. This little one grew quickly, ran about in and out of the lodge regardless of weather, and rarely listened to her mother. The mother tried to keep her daughter near her, to watch her, and keep her safe, but her daughter was impossible. She would climb tall trees to throw down pine cones. The daughter would swim in the fast waters to come back with fish in her mouth. Her daughter was not one to listen or learn from her mother. The daughter grew quickly into a woman.

One afternoon, the mother was out collecting firewood. Her daughter was now telling her about her dreams and her loneliness. The mother moved away from her daughter, gathering more and more firewood. The mother stopped suddenly, her daughter was talking to someone else. The voice that answered was that of a man. The mother dropped her wood and ran to her daughter's side. "Who were you speaking to? Was there a man here? Who was that?" Her daughter smiled at her. "I can talk to anyone I want to, but it is nice to know we are no longer alone here." That was all she would tell her mother.

In the morning, they went out to look for berries. The mother kept an eye on her daughter. The daughter slipped away out of her sight, but the mother heard her speaking again to the man. The mother quietly hid behind a tree and watched them. The man said, "This is the last time I shall visit you. I will not come again."

Her daughter laughed. The mother groaned for she knew all too well what was coming.

The daughter grew in size. Each day she got larger and larger. One night, the mother was awakened by the sound of boys' voices. She turned her head, the voices were coming from her daughter's belly. The mother crawled on her hands and knees over to her daughter who appeared to be asleep. One of the boy's voices said, "It is time for us to be out of this tight place. How do we get out of here?" Another voice said, "We have to go down this long tunnel to find light. You must hold your breath, move very slowly, and crawl out of the tunnel."

"No, I am not going down that long tunnel. You go first, but I am going to kick my way out of here. That tunnel is too small for my big head. You go first and if it works for you fine, but I will find my own way out of here."

The mother tried to shake her daughter awake. Her daughter wouldn't awaken, she was warm, she was breathing, but she wouldn't open her eyes. The mother spread her daughter's legs and there came a fine young baby boy. The boy was surprised to see her. The other boy was kicking and tearing inside to get out. Finally he ripped open his mother's armpit and shot out of her with a scream. His grandmother caught him before he hit the ground.

The boys' mother groaned as blood flowed from her body. She was dead. The boys' grandmother held them, staring at her beautiful dead daughter. The Grandmother held the two boys in her arms. "Which one of you killed her? Which one of you ripped her open to save your own discomfort?" The baby boy who had come from his mother's armpit pointed to the other boy. The Grandmother took the innocent, but accused baby boy, and threw him as far as she could away from the lodge. He landed in some grassy leaves. "You stay away from us. You killed your mother, and you are never to come near this lodge again as long as you live!"

Grandmother took the guilty baby into the lodge to feed him and care for him. Her daughter's body was placed on top of a mountain to watch the sun come up and go down day by day. The two boys grew quickly. One lived in the lodge, the other lived in the forest. Each day they met up with one another to play, hunt, catch fish, and challenge each other in games. Grandmother couldn't do anything about this for once outside they were faster than she was for she had aged and become more fragile. The boys ran the circuit of the island on the Grandfather's Turtle's back before old Grandmother could walk to the edge of the forest. Soon the boys grew into men. The boy that lived with grandmother called himself Flint for he had a quick wit and a sharp temper. Sapling was the name of the brother who lived alone in his own lodge.

One early morning, a man outside of Sapling's lodge called to him. Sapling met him, asking, "Who are you? There are no others here, but the three of us. Where did you come from?" The man smiled at him, saying, "Your father sent me to you. He asked me to bring you this bow and these arrows. Here in this basket are some corn kernels, use them wisely." The man turned and walked back into the forest. Sapling tried to follow him but the man was gone. Sapling took the bow and arrows and killed a bird for his dinner. That evening he roasted it on his fire.

Old Grandmother called Flint to her side as she started the evening fire. "Your brother is cooking something good. Smell it? Go to him and tell him that he must share it with us. I am his old grandmother and he should help us now." Flint ran through the forest to his brother's lodge. "Sapling, what is that you are cooking?" Sapling smiled at his brother. "It is a bird that I shot with my new bow and arrows." Flint looked at the bow and arrows. "Those are nice. Where did you get them from? Did you make them?"

"No," Sapling said. "A man brought them to me. He said they were a gift from my father." Flint smiled. "Well, now maybe we can find out who our father is. Maybe he has some gifts for me, too." Sapling shook his head. "No, as long as you live with Grandmother the man won't visit you." Flint glared at his brother. "What do you mean?" Sapling sighed. "The tall man said that grandmother will spoil the food I catch, she will spoil you, and life here will not be good as long as she is here." Flint returned to his grandmother's lodge, but he said nothing.

The next evening, old grandmother called Flint. "Smell that? That is your brother cooking up something good again. Go to him and ask him for some of it?" Flint shook his head, "No, you go. Yesterday he said he would not share with us." Grandmother shoved Flint aside to march over to Sapling's lodge. "Sapling, what is it that you are roasting there!"

"Grandmother, I am roasting corn. Go away. I will not give you any. Go away!"

Grandmother stood her ground. "Sapling, you come out here and talk to me. Where did you get that corn? Sapling, come out here and talk to me!"

"Grandmother, no, I will not talk to you. You threw me out of the lodge where I was born, you would not help me when I was growing and now that a man has brought me food from my father, I will not share it with you. Go away!"

Grandmother stamped her foot. "Sapling, you can give me at least one kernel of that corn. Just throw out one kernel of the corn! One kernel of the corn will not hurt you. Let me taste just one little bit!"

Sapling called out to her, "No, I cannot do it. If I give you one piece of corn, one kernel, the corn will be ruined for all time. You will spoil it!"

Grandmother pushed back the blanket of his lodge. She reached down and grabbed up a handful of dirt and threw it on the fire. The pot holding the boiling corn overflowed as the dirt filled the pot. "There, is that what you want?" She kicked ashes on the roasting meat over the pot. "Is this what you want to eat? If you do not share then no one shall eat well."

Sapling stared at her, then at the fire of spoiled food. "Why did you do that? Why did you destroy something that was not yours to have?" He reached down to pick up a kernel of corn. "Now, when mankind wants corn they shall have to plant it in the dirt." Sapling pushed over a flat rock and threw the kernel on it. He knelt down to grind it into powder with another rock, "Now they will have to grind the corn with rocks like those you have kicked into my pot." He took the corn powder into his palm and held it out to her. "Now this is the corn meal that all women will make from now on, all because of you!"

Grandmother knelt down and with her fingers she pulled out the corn from the dirty pot. She took a clean pot full of water and put it back on the fire. She placed the kernels into the water pot over the fire. "Fine," she said. "This is the way it will be. If you say this is the way it must be, then this is how it will be."

Sapling glared at her. "Stop it, and just stop it. You aren't helping, just stop and leave this place." Grandmother hoisted up her skirts and left him alone. Sapling then decided he needed to explore this land of his father. Sapling traveled from coast to coast, finding new mud. He mixed the mud into shapes of animals and then blew on them. These shapes came alive, new birds flew in the sky, new types of animals hunted at night, and new types of fish swam around their little island. Sapling found great joy in making things come to life.

Flint noticed the new animals and birds. He became increasingly jealous of his brother. He knew his brother had different powers than he did, but he did not want his brother to have this much control over the life on the island. Flint formed a cave in the side of a mountain and promptly set out trapping the animals to hide them in the cave. Flint fed them at first, but soon this job was too troublesome. Flint found a huge rock which he pushed it in front of the cave. The animals were now completely trapped there was no food, no water, no fresh air for them.

In the morning, Sapling noticed that there were fewer birds in the sky. He called to the birds overhead, but they were afraid of him. This made him worried. He went into the forest to search for his wild deer and elk. There were none there. Sapling walked the whole island searching for his animals and finally he found the cave with the rock in front of it. Sapling used all his strength to push the rock just enough distance to let the animals out two-by-two. Sapling ran down the mountain calling the animals by name, hoping that they would find strength to push their way outside.

Flint saw the birds flying free. He quickly ran up the mountain to find the rock had been moved. Flint pushed the rock back in place, keeping the animals in there forever, allowing them to become the animals of the night caves. Flint hurried back to grandmother to warn her that times were going to change.

Sapling continued to call the animals to him. He decided to move them to the far side of the island. There at his lodge was a strange man who called out to Sapling, "Who are you?"

"I am Sapling." Sapling studied the man. "Who are you?"

The strange man smiled. "I am the maker of life here."

Sapling laughed. "No, you're not, I am the maker of life."

The two men walked around each other. Finally, Sapling said, "Move that mountain to be behind us."

The strange man looked at the mountain. "Certainly." He took Sapling by the arm and turned him around. "Now, the mountain is behind us."

Sapling laughed. "No that was not what I meant. You only turned us around, I want you to move the mountain." The man shook his head. "I can't move that mountain." Sapling patted him on the back. "Then you are not the maker of life, are you?"

The man frowned. "No, I guess not."

As the two men walked back to Sapling's lodge the mid-day sky unexpectedly grew dark. They hurried to Grandmother's lodge. Flint was standing outside. Flint greeted his brother. "What is happening, why is it dark all of a sudden?"

The strange man held out his hand to keep Flint from falling over a stone. "It is dark because someone has removed your mother's head. Your mother's head held the light of life. She was a daughter of the land of Tooth which brought light to the world. Someone has taken her head and we must find it quickly." Sapling called to the animals of night. Carefully, the animals guided the three men up the side of the mountain. When they got to the place of their mother's body, they found Grandmother. She was cutting her daughter's body up into pieces and flinging them into the sky. Parts of the body became stars, other parts of their mother's body became flying meteors crashing into the earth. Grandmother was screaming and crying that she had been left behind to suffer with her miserable grandsons. She held up an accusing finger and said, "You are both like your mother, just like your mother!" Grandmother fell and died.

Sapling reached down, finally touching his grandmother's hands. The man stared at him. Sapling shook his head. "This was the first time I have been able to touch the old woman since I was an infant. She threw me out of the lodge when I was an infant." The man pulled him back. "Now you must go and find your mother's head for it holds the light of the sun. People are coming, they will need the sun to live. Go and return with the sun." Sapling nodded and ran down the mountain in search of the sun.

Sapling called on the help of Kingfisher to help him fly high into the sky. They found no sign of Sun. Kingfisher placed Sapling on the ground. He asked Raccoon to help him find his mother's head of light. Raccoon took him to Beaver who had seen the head of light fall into a pond. Yellowhammer guided Sapling in a canoe to the area. Otter swam out to guide the canoe. Soon they came to dull light on a small island. Fox was standing under the tree which held the light of the sun. Kingfisher flew up into the tree and knocked the head free. Fox caught the head of light and brought it to Sapling. Sapling threw the head up high into the sky to become Sun. "Now, you shall be the sun and shine brightly over the land of all of your children. You can pass under the island at night to rest and the moon shall show us the light of night. Be at peace, my mother, you shall light up the sky for all time."

Sapling took the canoe back to the main island. There he knelt on the mud of the shore and created a man being. He laid it out to rest in the sun while he created a woman being. He breathed into the woman being and she came alive. Sapling took the man being and breathed into his mouth and he came alive. The two ran into the forest to hide from him. Sapling frowned at them. The man appeared next to Sapling. "They have to hide from you for you are huge, strong, and terrifying to them. Let them be for they will have children. They will tell them of you and your greatness. Leave them alone."

Sapling walked with the man as he told him of his brother Flint. "Flint is busy at work on the far side of the mountain. We don't know what he is doing and he won't show anyone what he is making. It would be good for you to go and talk with him." Sapling waited until the next morning. He walked on the beach, hearing People's voices in the forest. They were bearing children and learning of life. Sapling stayed away from them.

Finally, he found his brother. "Flint, what are you doing over here? I thought we would work together to make life here." Flint shook his head and would not show him what he was doing. Sapling pulled Flint aside and stared. There in front of Flint were horrible monsters with People heads but bodies of beasts and horrible monsters. "What are you doing, Flint? What are these beings?"

Flint glared at him. "These are to protect the forest. If People become too many they will spoil life here. These will keep the People from taking over the earth." Sapling pulled down a tree branch and crushed the horrible figures. Some fled away into the forest, but most of them were killed. "You cannot do this, Flint, we are here to provide a good life for beings, not a painful life."

Flint turned and pushed his brother to the ground. "You do not know me, you do not know what I need! You only think about the others. What about what I need! Who will take care of me now that Grandmother is dead? Who? Who will feed me, wash me, and find food for me? Who? Not you!" Flint ran down the beach.

Sapling ran after his brother and caught him by the arm. "Flint, you can take care of yourself. You can make your own life! Don't do this!" Flint shoved his brother aside. "You don't care about anyone but yourself!"

Sapling stopped his brother by holding him firmly. He dug a deep pit in the sand with his free hand. Sapling jerked Flint into the pit, yelling "Why must you always want to do what is easy even if it hurts you in the end? Flint, we will meet up again and then we can work together, but you need to find out how strong you are by yourself first!"

Sapling filled the pit with dirt, leaving Flint isolated way down in the center of the earth. It was dark and cold. Flint built himself a fire, which then he could not put out, but by its light he found that he could take the roots of many of the plants and trees and turn them into deadly herbs.

In time, People grew strong and no longer needed Sapling to help them. Sapling went down to the beach and dug up the location of his brother's pit. Flint had gone. He was no longer there. Flint had moved to a different location. He had grown pale and quiet. He had nothing more to ever say to his brother.

Sapling moved up into the sky to watch over the earth. When they became sick, he taught them medicine. The People told him of the roots and plants they found that would kill them or make them sick. Sapling smiled, he knew his brother was still alive and working against him. Sometimes Sapling has everything in control and at other times Flint has People at war. If we wait, life comes back into harmony.

The term Iroquoian is derived from the name Iroquois, a name adopted from the Algonquian Indian language by the early French explorers in the 1600-1800s.

There were actually five tribes that united into a permanent confederacy for offense and defense against the incoming colonists and raiding tribes. They inhabited the central and eastern portions of the region now within the State of New York. They had other names such as the Five Nations or the League of the Iroquois. They adopted the Tuscaroras in 1722 to become the Six Nations. These original five tribes came to their height during the latter part of the 17th Century. This union allowed them to dominate the greater watershed of the Great Lakes region. They never had large numbers of population, but had great diplomacy which was an effective political organization set up with maternal blood relationships, both real and mythological. It was believed by the United States government, in the 1700s, that the Six Nations had a superior mentality and an ability to understand the politics of that era.

Prickly Granddaughters / Pima

Carol Many Feathers shrugged when I asked her to repeat her name. "This isn't my real name. Can't give you my real name, but this was a name that they used to call me at the Mission School back in nineteen fifty-three." She wrapped her granddaughter's braids around her fingers as the young girl of nine sat in her lap. "I tell this story to my girls. They should know the stories of the old ones just in case the television gets broken, Hah, hah, hah!"

The nine year old squirmed in her grandmother's lap. Carol took her hand. "Don't worry, nothing is going to happen to your television! But you listen to this story and tell me if this isn't better than television, okay?" Carol leaned back on the park bench, hugging her granddaughter as she told us this story.

[This story is consistent with research from the Bureau of American Ethnology.]

The Story
of
Prickly Granddaughters

"My daughter, it is time for you to get up and help with the chores, get up and get moving!" The elderly mother poked at her daughter with a stick. Her daughter didn't move, she only groaned. "Mother, I don't feel well, I'm tired, leave me alone. Go away."

The mother continued to poke her daughter. "You are the youngest of seven children, yet you act older than any of them. They are married, have children, are busy with their lives and you just do nothing! What is wrong with you?"

The daughter sat up and pushed the stick away from her. "Mother, there is nothing I can do that would be done as well as my brothers and sisters. There is nowhere I can go where they haven't already been. I have nothing to achieve. I'm not of any value. Leave me alone."

Her mother stormed out of the mud house to the olla (water jar). She filled a ladle with water, marched back inside to her daughter, and threw the water at her. "Get up! There are chores to do for me if not for yourself. I am your mother, an old woman who has had a good life and now you are here, you take care of me!"

The dripping water did not help the daughter's mood. "Mother, go away, go away and die or just go away and live with someone else, pick another one of your children to torment. Just leave me alone!" The mother took hold of her daughter's arm and pulled her out of the mud hut. "There, look at the sun, look at the trees, the birds, the earth. They are waiting for you to get up and get to work." The mother dropped her daughter's arm to walk into the hut. The daughter's bedroll, moccasins, and hair brush were brought to her. "Here, you want to sleep, you can do it outside during the day and inside during the night. There!" Her mother dumped the things on her daughter.

"All right, I'm up." The young woman shook out her bedroll. "What do you want me to do?"

Her mother gave her a, "Harrumpf!"

"I'll go get more water and help you with the willows." The daughter picked up an empty olla to walk down the path to the stream.

Mother waited for her daughter to return. She waited all day. She wasn't going to hunt her down. At least her daughter was up, did something, and was not unconscious in the hut. Mother turned her head, no sound came from the path except the chirping of birds in the trees. Her gnarled fingers twisted the maguey fiber round and round, weaving it into a loose rope. She had finished off three long ropes for trade and now she was starting on the martynia pods. She made a 'bee' out of it, removing the fiber by breaking the hooked end and holding it in her teeth while the split fiber was pulled off with her fingers. She stripped the fibers, pulling them straight to place them at her knees. Tending the fire to heat up the olla of water, she poured the hot water on the stripped pods which made it simpler to separate the fiber from the pod. These fibers, once free, were placed into coils.

Mother sat working, patiently waiting for her daughter to return, her pile of agave leaves that her daughter was to work on, reminded her that she needed to get the jar shaped grain baskets ready for her son's feast day. Taking the arrow bush, she dumped it into the hot water, making it more supple. Slowly she wrapped it round and round making a checker-weave shallow basket bowl. Later, she would coil clay, using this shallow basket as the foundation of the bowl.

Sun was setting, the air was becoming cooler, and Mother picked up the olla. Pouring the dirty water out onto the earth, she lifted it to refill it at the small stream. Perhaps there she would find her daughter. The walk helped Mother straighten her back, clear her head from all the thoughts and worry of her daughter, and allowed her to come upon her by chance.

There, just getting out of the water was her daughter. "What are you doing in the stream, my daughter?"

Her daughter was startled to hear another voice. "Oh, Mother, it is you? I was washing, cleaning off the sadness that was within me. The water helped me feel better. Now I am ready to help with the chores."

Mother leaned over, hearing her back creaking, she frowned. "Daughter, the day is done. I have woven rope to trade for material. We can get you some new cloth for your brother's feast day dance. Also, I started in on the basket coils for you to finish tomorrow. The sun is going down, now it is time to eat our dinner and rest." Her daughter playfully took the filled olla from her mother. "Here, let me carry this for you. I have the other one here, oops, it broke by accident this morning when I dropped it."

Mother studied the shattered olla. It was not dropped, it was smashed to pieces. She thought it best to say nothing. The two women quietly returned to the cooking fire pit. Daughter fixed the meal while Mother sat and watched. The evening was spent in silence as they both went into the hut to sleep.

The next morning, Mother awoke to find her daughter gone. Daughter was not outside the hut, she was not by the stream, she was gone. There were chores to do, obligations to meet, responsibilities to fulfill. Mother worked hard all day to meet these. That evening, she ate her dinner cold and waited. Finally, she crawled into hut and went to sleep. The next day and the day after, there was no news of her daughter. Mother thought of walking to her older daughter's house to see if she had gone there, but the two of them hadn't spoken in a long time. She doubted her youngest would go to all that trouble. Mother decided that her daughter was busy finding her purpose.

Winter came and with it the cold winds. Mother's back was bitterly cold all the time, but she managed to find enough wood for the fire. When the winter solstice came, her oldest son arrived with two fine horses to take her to his village. "You should have let me know that you were in need, I would have come to get you sooner!" Her son helped her on the horse. Mother smiled at him. "Son, I am old, but not helpless. Being at your home this cold winter will be a nice relief." No one spoke of the youngest daughter all that winter.

In the warmth of spring, Mother was returned to her hut. She was anxious to get back to her way of life. She missed her personal things and the sounds of her own home. Her son helped her gather a huge pile of wood. Ollas of water were filled and placed near the hut while he hunted for two days to be sure she had plenty of food. There was no sign of her youngest daughter. Finally, her son had to return to his family.

Spring fed into summer. Fawns from the high country came down to drink from the stream. Birds chirped and nested all around her little hut. Mother was pleased that her life was good, but she wondered about her youngest daughter. People visited from time-to-time to trade or share news. Mother never mentioned youngest daughter for that would show weakness.

It was in the fall, just as the winds were starting to blow across the desert, when she returned. Daughter was there in the morning, by the cook fire, she was stirring porridge. Mother nodded to her as her daughter held out a bowl of porridge for her. "Mother, I have come home, but only for a short time. You shall have a gift from me, a gift of life." Daughter pulled back her shawl to show her large belly. Mother gasped. "You are with child? Where is your man?"

Daughter burst out laughing. "I have no man! It's just me." Mother said nothing, she ate her porridge. Four days later, the daughter gave birth to twin girls. Mother hurried to the stream to get ollas of water, when she returned, her daughter was gone. Two little baby girls wrapped tightly in warm blankets slept by the fire. This was Mother's gift, this was all.

These two grew quickly. Grandmother had become the center of their lives. Grandmother was a quick and quiet woman with her stooped shoulders, long black braids, and gnarled fingers. The two sisters grew tall and strong as they were taught the ways of the people, they were included in all the ceremonies. Grandmother's matriarchal line was strong in this group, her father and grandfather had been fine hunters and warriors. Her mother and grandmother had healed many sick and brought many babies to life. Grandmother never appeared to waver from her duties.

As the granddaughters grew, they appeared to be more interested in what the other daughter owned, or was given, than the chores they needed to do. Each time a relative came to visit, they would bring gifts to the granddaughters and some food for Grandmother. This was their way of helping the family. The next morning though, the girls would quarrel and fight over each other's gifts, leaving grandmother to carry the water from the stream, chop the wood for the cooking fires, and gather willows to weave baskets.

Every morning, Grandmother would grind the wheat and corn to make porridge. But on this one morning, Grandmother told them as she put the olla on the fire outside of the house. "No fighting today. When you fight you disturb the water. Most mornings, while you fight the water goes foul from your arguing. This cannot go on for then I have to send one of you down to get more water. Both of you quarrel if I pick one over the other for the work. This morning, we need to agree to no more fighting."

The granddaughters stared at their grandmother. The tallest spoke first. "Grandmother, we're not fighting. We just talk about what nice things my little sister has while I have nothing of any value. She has been given everything beautiful and I just get old goods that nobody else wants. We're just discussing these things."

The shorter sister pouted. "Me! You're the one who receives the nice gifts! You're everybody's favorite! I'm just an afterthought, I'm just the one who is the burden, no one likes me! They just do what is traditional, they don't care about me! You're the pretty one, you're the one who will have grandmother's ceremonial dress when she dies! I'm just a nobody!"

The taller sister shoved her finger into her shorter sister's face. "Every nice gift that I was ever given, you take and destroy! Every time I do something, you have to try and do better. Well, you're not better than me, you will never be better than me. You're just a little smelly dead rat. Why don't you just go away?"

The shorter granddaughter ran to her sister and shoved her toward the fire. Sparks flew landing on the wood pile. Grandmother threw some water on the sisters. "You both are to blame for this arguing. Stop it right now! How can you say such hateful things to each other? You are both completely different from the other person. My taller granddaughter, you like to dream and watch the river drift by, making up stories of the animals and the fish you bring home for dinner. My little one, you are busy all the time, drawing, sewing, and helping me with the grinding of the corn. How can you say that one is better than the other? You are two different people!"

Grandmother pulled the olla of porridge off the fire. "Here, now eat your porridge. The water has turned because of you, eat it anyway, this is all your fault." The two sisters stormed off to go in their own direction. Grandmother did the chores, shaking her head sorrowfully, how could these girls find a husband when they were both so greedy and self-centered.

The following morning, the sky was overcast. The hot sun was taking a rest from heating the earth. Grandmother was coming back from the stream with an olla of water when she heard the two sisters arguing again. Grandmother put down the olla. The sisters should be thinking of weaving ceremonial dresses. Their thoughts should be about finding a man for marriage. Instead all they focused on was each other. Grandmother walked over to a mesquite bush to pull off a long switch of a barbed branch. Walking hurriedly up the hill to the granddaughters, Grandmother flicked the barbed mesquite switch back and forth. The sisters didn't see her for they were yelling in each other's faces.

Grandmother reached out for the tallest granddaughter, and then she flung angrily at the shorter. The mesquite barbs drew blood on their backs and legs. The two sisters quickly diverted their attention to Grandmother. "What are you doing? Why are you whipping us?" Grandmother now was whipping their defensive arms. "I have had it with both of you! Your duties are to be women who should marry, help the community, yet all you do is argue with each other. Enough!" Grandmother lashed out with all of her strength. The two granddaughters ran away from her. They ran down the hill, jumped over the small stream and into the desert. Grandmother ran after them, panting and waving the mesquite branch in front of her.

The tallest stopped at the edge of the mountain. "I shall turn into a Saguaro, so I shall last forever and bear fruit every summer. l don't want to live with people, I don't want to live with a man. I shall stand here forever and be helpful in my own way!" She turned toward her sister to become a Saguaro.

The shorter sister laughed. "I can do better than you. You are nothing compared to me! I shall turn into a Palo Verde Tree and stand here forever, longer than you! These hills and mountains are so bare that I shall give them color. They shall be green because of me! You can stand alone, but I shall be greater than you!" There she became a Palo Verde Tree.

Grandmother hurried to catch up with the girls, and then stopped when she heard whispering, "I am greater than you!"

"No, you're not. Why is it that everything I do, you have to do?"

"Because, I can do things better than you!"

Grandmother turned her head, there she saw the tall saguaro cactus and a Palo Verde Tree. Grandmother ran to the Saguaro, hugging it she cried out, "My granddaughters, no, this is not what 1 wanted for you! You are both beautiful, you are my life! No!"

The Saguaro cactus' spines punctured Grandmother, all the way to her heart. She fell down dead at the foot of the two plants. This is how the Saguaro and the Palo Verde Trees came to be. They are still there and if you are very quiet, you can hear them still arguing.

The Pima Indians live in the central southern part of the state of Arizona. Frank Russell wrote of the Pima Indians in 1904. His collected works hold the beliefs of the Pima told to him by Ka'mal t Kak or Thin Man who was the most popular of the few remaining narrators of speeches. Since Russell's work, many have recorded stories of the Pima. Carol called him the Thin Man and that in his prime Thin Man stood at over six feet tall. Thin Man was known as a teacher of beliefs and making weaving looms.

The term Pima comes from the Spanish, the natives themselves use the name Otama or Ohotoma. Carol informed me that when they are at home, the people refer to their own group as the A'-a'tam or 'the people.' This term distinguishes them from the Papago. The Pima were ruthlessly attacked by the Apache. They felt the Apache, who like the Pima were also basket makers, had an ability to provoke spirits of terror and death. Living on the edge of the desert allowed the Pima to become incredibly creative with their irrigation of corn fields, beans, wild grasses and fields of wheat. In the 1800s colonists wanted their land. In May, 1901, President McKinley visited Phoenix, Arizona. Pima people knew of no boundaries between Mexico and the United States until the United States Army intervened to put them onto reservations. There they did well until Phoenix grew too large for the water supply. The state of Arizona dammed the rivers to provide more water for the cities and the Pima, Papago, and Maricopa had to do without water. Many died. Pima now suffer from diabetes, high blood pressure, and alcoholism. Carol explained that the People need to work the land that is their way, not to just sit on it and wait to die with food stamps.

Food made from the Plants on the Pima Reservation:

Shelled corn was ground on the metate and baked in large cakes in the ashes. Corn was boiled with ashes, dried in the hulls then thoroughly dried and parched with coals or over the fire. It was also ground into gruel, but was not as good as wheat pinole.

I'savik: thorns of cactus gathered and eaten raw.

I'untany, Atriplex in Spanish: the heads of the salt bush are pounded in the mortar and screened to separate the hulls. The seeds were washed, spread to dry, parched with a piece of olla and ground on the metate. They were ready to be eaten as pinole, or dry if one was really hungry.

Ka'ifsa, Cicer Arietinum Linn: the chick pea was raised in small quantities and was purchased from traders. This is the garbanzo bean from Mexico.

Kaf, Chenopodium murale: the seed was gathered early in the summer and was prepared by parching and grinding, after this it was eaten as pinole or combined with other meals.

Ka'meuvat: after the August rain the seed was gathered, parched over coals in the parching pan, ground on the metate, and eaten as pinole.

Kan'yo: Sorghum is cultivated when the water supply allows, it has been brought in by traders and used in most meals.

Ki'ak: the heads of the annual plant are gathered and seeds beaten with a kiaha stick used as a flail. The seeds are moistened, parched and it looks like popcorn, eaten with plenty of water.

Koi, Prosopis velutina: mesquite beans were the most important part of the diet in primitive times. Most livestock today eat this, but it was the main staple of the early ones.

Me'la- watermelons are one of the most important crops of the Pima people. They are eaten about six months out of the year.

Naf' or Opuntia englmanni: the thorns are brushed off the fruit of the prickly pear before it is gathered. It is then peeled and eaten, the seeds are thrown away. The fruit can cause fever in those not used to eating it.

Saguaro of the Pima: the dried fruit or the plant is boiled and the liquid is used in making a drink during famine.

O':sotc I'wuptpat: the black berry of this thorny bush is gathered in basket bowls after it has been beaten down with sticks. It can be eaten raw and the seeds are thrown away.

Rsat: the bulb of the wild onion is eaten, it is common at the foot of the Estrellas.

Tcaia'aolt, Echinocactus wislizeni: the pulp of this is valuable to those who are dying of thirst. It is eaten after being cut into strips and boiled all day. It can be boiled with mesquite beans, a layer of each in the cooking pot. It can be boiled with sugar from cactus flowers. It is eaten as a confection among visitors and outsiders who trade with the Papago.

Hot and Cold Brothers / Coeur D'alene

In the northwest, the beginning land of the First People was surrounded by water. There was water on all sides which lapped at the land with a gentle tongue. It was believed that the land of the First People was new and built just for them. Before the people arrived there was water everywhere. The land and the life upon it came from the First Woman Spirit who grew out of the Waters of Life.

In the beginning, there was only a handful of First People. They had a difficult time for there was little food, no shelter, and they had no knowledge of how to survive. The winds blew down their temporary shelters and the sun killed their small gardens. The First People did not know how to keep alive until Coyote came. Coyote showed the First People how to catch salmon and dry it for the long winter months. Coyote only did this for a small fee of fifty percent of the salmon.

Coyote explained to the First People how to plant gardens and showed them how to develop irrigation and ponds to keep fresh water available for their plants. He only flooded three small villages while explaining this technique. Coyote felt the First People had very little excitement in their lives, so he taught them art. He showed them how to draw, of course his drawings could not be shown to children, but the First People learned how to draw designs and symbols of gratitude to Coyote. The First People liked drawing so much that they drew all over their bodies, on pieces of bark, and on dried animals' skins.

There was a time when the winds were so strong that the island was blown around in the waters and many people were lost. Coyote made a snare and trapped the wind, keeping it in a bag he slung it over his shoulder. Many times when Coyote fell asleep the wind would escape, but somehow Coyote could catch it in time to get his salmon dinners and listen to the songs the First People sang about him.

Two spirit brothers moved over the island. They noticed that Coyote was doing well for himself with the First People These two brothers thought of getting some satisfaction for them. The two brothers were called Heat and Cold. Heat was very good-looking and had no trouble at all getting the First People to accept him. The First People were unsure of Cold for when he spoke fog came out of his mouth and he was extremely ugly with wrinkled, dry skin that flaked off everywhere he went.

The two brothers worked in harmony with the First People, who showed their appreciation by bringing them food, singing them songs, and drawing great artistic designs for them. The First People made it a rule that they would never invite one Spirit Brother without the other for playing favorites would certainly get them in trouble. Besides none of them knew how to speak to Cold Brother without shivering, this they felt would offend him.

In the summer the people built a long communal lodge for special gatherings or for celebrations to show their appreciation for the two brothers. In fair weather, the long lodge was a single one-sided lean-to, with fires built in the front. Sometimes the people put up windbreaks of mats or even brush to protect it from harsh winds. When Cold brother brought hard storms or cold winters, the people would move into a Long House.

The Long House was made from tall poles that were cut to build the frame walls. Excavation was done by all the people at the direction of the chief or elders. The building of the Long House was a community matter and a public duty. The butt ends of the poles were sharpened to catch in the ground, but stones were used and placed against the butt of each pole. Some people used mats inside the lodges around their heads of their beds to protect them from those walking around at night. These carefully braided mats were tied to the poles and intended for protection against draught at the base of the lodge. Mats also helped to push the draught toward the smoke hole to draw the smoke out. The people also learned how to make sweat houses with a common dome-shaped frame of bent willows for cleansing when Cold brother blew his ice wind.

In the summertime, when Heat brother was at his hottest, bark shelters of the single lean-to type were used. Because of the wet weather that came between the Heat brother's time and the Cold brother's time -the people built scaffolds for the storing of their skins and other goods, to keep them dry. Anything else of value was covered with mats and placed on high shelves. The people were good at weaving baskets, mats, and using poles and frames for stretching skins and drying berries and meats.

Heat brother called to the people and asked them make him a special robe. Heat brother was tired of wearing only his moccasins, long leggings, belt, breechclout, shirt and headband. He ordered, "I want a tanned soft robe made from the skins of elk, deer, fawn, buffalo, marmot, ground squirrel, and beaver. Ah, and a collar of coyote, lynx, and other animals all sewn together with sinew or bark thread."

Heat brother told them, "I want this fine robe to have layers of fringe with ornaments of the sun sewn into it." The people did as they were asked out of fear of being burned by Heat brother.

Cold brother heard his brother's call for a robe. Cold brother looked down at his arms covered with tattoos of geometric winter animals mixed with the realistic figures of snow and ice. Cold brother called down to the people. "I need to have a ground squirrel robe with at least eighty skins sewn together. This is to be one piece of my two piece robe for the other piece is to be the skin of a year-old buffalo sewn together with ground squirrel skins, with crosswise bands of beads or quill designs. I want the base of this to have narrow twisted stripes of muskrat skins painted with designs of thick dark clouds and symbols of snow and ice."

When the brothers received their robes they were pleased, but Heat Brother felt that he needed to go on a vacation and show off his fine robe. Heat brother studied his robe with admiration, saying to his brother, "You stay here and watch these people. Don't let them get too cold. Don't over work them for they are fragile. I shall be back in time."

Cold brother hovered over the island. He spent most of his time studying his beautiful two piece robe. There was something about it that displeased him, but he couldn't figure out what. He called to several of the women and asked them to make the quill designs larger. They did as he asked. Cold brother strutted around with his fancy layered robe, but somehow he felt uneasy. Finally he decided that his problem was his dislike for the First People. He was tired of them, tired of their ways, tired of watching them. Also, he knew that the First People were frightened of him, they didn't trust him. He wasn't invited to the salmon run, as he was when his brother was around, nor did the people invite him to their dances or their celebrations.

Cold Brother became angry and decided that he would kill the First People. He blew cold wind, followed by cold falling sleet, and ended by dropping heavy, wet, freezing snow on the First People. They huddled in their villages, trying to keep the fires going, but the wood was wet. Many people died. Messengers were sent to announce the death to the neighbors and to relatives living a distance away. The corpses were prepared for burial when Cold brother was resting. Poles were made into a stretcher with the poles sewn into the robe. This stretcher allowed the men to lift the dead onto their shoulders and carry the body outside to suspend it from a tree branch until relatives arrived and people could gather to sing and chant the spirit away.

If Cold brother allowed them a period of four days, the body would be taken up into some cliffs or laid out away from the village in a snowy arroyo to be buried. Very little of the dead person's property was buried with him, most times it was so cold that they buried him in his robe with the poles still in it.

The cries and the prayers of the First People who were on the verge of freezing reached Heat brother. He hurried to return. Heat brother blew away the clouds of cold snow. He pushed back and melted the thick snow banks into rolling rivers. Almost all of the crops were spoiled or destroyed. Many of the diggers and pickers were dead or had lost limbs. The people spent their time making rattles to hang over their doors to shake away ghosts. Many families had perished and their lodges were completely removed after being fumigated. Those who helped with the dead had to fast for several days and wash themselves in running water. The close family members would scratch their own necks to reflect the pain over the loss of loved ones.

Heat Brother watched in anger as the women cut their hair short, men fasted for days, and children's faces were covered with ash every morning and washed off every evening. Heat brother's anger grew and grew as he watched the people in their suffering. Cold brother hid from his brother. Heat brother let his warmth melt the snow, allowed the people to go to the sweat lodges, and gave the people time to recover.

The First People were relieved at first, but then the weather got hotter and hotter. Heat brother made the weather so hot that he killed Cold brother. The First People gathered together and begged and pleaded for Heat brother to bring back Cold brother for they would surely die in such heat. Heat brother agreed. "People, it is for you to now know that heat can always kill the cold, melt the ice, steam away the frost, and turn snow banks into running rivers. The cold may come to keep the land still and allow it to rest. The cold may let you gather together and rest your backs from the hard work of summer. Cold allows you to be with your families to share stories and learn tradition, but never forget the heat will come again. It will not leave you to suffer in cold."

The two brothers lived together now over the island which has grown into the Big Land. The Heat brother watches over the Cold brother with a careful eye. Cold brother knows that his Heat brother can kill him and remains moderately good most of the time. There still are horrible winters in the Northwest and a very hot summer with rain but everyone knows that this is just the brothers testing each other.

In 1904, the Coeur d'Alene covered the area from British Columbia to the states of Washington and Montana. They were related to the Salishan dialect group and were nomadic most of the time due to the inclement winter weather and the hot, humid weather of summer. There are different versions of this tale, where the Cold brother went away first and the Heat brother cooked everyone until Cold brother returned to save the people. It is true historically that many people froze to death in the extreme winters and at times the summers were unbearably humid.

My storyteller tells me there were no beliefs related to the creation of light and dark. The sun was Robin, the bird, sent up to give the people light during the day. Robin became tired and flew too close, people had to jump into the water to survive the heat. Robin was replaced by a one-eyed man who remains above the earth at a safe distance. The use of brothers in this story reflects the male competition. It was not uncommon for two brothers to try and out hunt or out run the other. They worked hard to earn more tattoos than other males in the group.

Tree Brothers / Flathead

Martin Letener stood tall outside of the grocery store near the turn off to Belen, New Mexico. I met him as I came outside with two cherry popsicles. We had both agreed that the hundred degree heat merited a cherry popsicle. He pushed back his black felt hat, pulled the paper off the popsicle, and smiled. "Hey, ya. You know the Flathead were called the Salish, Selish, and Sale'ed up until they decided they wanted to have their own name." The red juice of the popsicle started to run down his hand as he sucked at the tip of it. "Whoa, these are good, but they are melting really fast!"

Handing him a napkin from my pocket, he smiled. "Well, we decided to call ourselves Tete Platte which is the French name, it is a strange name, but it was ours. My grandfather said the name was given to them by traders who came to live with the old ones, but in sign language it was interpreted as one who was "pressed side of the head" or "pressed head." He handed me the dripping red napkin.

"The Upper Kutenai claim that the tribe was named Flathead for Wide Head people. It was thought that the people had pressed heads, but no one pressed their heads. That is ridiculous. The exact original location is not known today, although some anthropologists who know more than the people they study seem to think the place where we came from was around Jocko or Bitterroot Valley in the western main range of the Rocky Mountains." Martin took the popsicle stick and threw it in the round white oil container used for garbage. "My grandmother called us the Leg People. She said that they remained in the country where the Wide Head lived, but the Flat Head name stayed with our people."

Martin pulled a pack of Marlboro cigarettes out of his pocket and opened it. He tilted toward me. "No," I said quietly. "Do you mind if I smoke, it is a native tradition, don't you know?' I just smiled.

"So, the Distant Plains tribes got in the habit of calling all the people in that region Flat Heads or Wide Heads and in a general way this was adopted by the fur traders of the early 1800s. Kids today who have family in the military choose to cut their hair flat on top. This is their tradition!" He motioned with his fingers over his head. "All right, now that you know who we are, let me tell you the story of the Tree Brothers."

The Story of Tree Brothers

The Flathead people believe that there are three worlds, one above the other, the middle one being the earth on which the people live. All of this started with the two chiefs who were brothers. There was the great and good chief brother who was the source of life and lived in the upper world. This older brother, Amo'tken was the great chief who made rain and snow, he made everything right on the earth and in the sky. Amo'tken brought food to the people and they prayed to him.

Amt'p was the mysterious younger brother. In his strange unknown manner, he would bring droughts or diseases to the crops. If he was in a terrible mood, he would kill off all the wild game, leaving the people to starve. Amt'p was chief of the underworld which he ruled with a nasty attitude all the time. No one prayed to Amt'p, at least not on purpose for all spirits wicked and cruel lived with him. If they heard a person's voice they would enter into their being through their mouth to take over their spirit. Amt'p lived below the ground around the roots of the great tree and it is there where the earth is filled with mildew, molds, and fungus that grow under the skin.

It is believed that the two brothers decided to have a contest. This contest was about knocking down the Great Tree of Life. Amo'tken climbed the tree believing that with his weight of goodness and light, the tree would fall to the ground. While Amo'tken was climbing the tree, his younger brother Amt'p was burrowing under the tree securing the roots of the tree into great depths of the ground. Once the older brother was in the top of the tree, he started jumping on it, yelling at it, and trying to get it to topple, but Amt'p had a secure hold. The fat, thick, wonderful tree with many branches of fields, mountains, valleys, and running rivers did not budge. It did not move. It held fast.

Older brother Amo'tken knew that if he left the tree, his brother Amt'p could pull up the roots and toss the tree aside to win the contest. Amt'p realized that if he were to come up from under the tree, the tree roots would pull lose and the tree would fall, allowing his older brother to win the contest. Neither one of them was going to move from their position. The tree stayed upright.

For all time the Great Chief Am'tk-en sits on the top of the tree, while his brother the bad chief Amt'p lives in the roots of the tree, deep within the earth. All the good people, when they die, follow the streams north and then west to the spirit land where they will sit in the top of the tree which has lands great and beautiful. The east is the region of birth and life, the west that of death and mystery. The people who are nasty and cruel, steal, murder, and lie go the land of Amt'p where they are made to suffer and lie awake, listening for eternity in the dark. These two brothers are both stubborn and shall remain with this tree for all time.

The Flathead are closely related to those of the Plateau tribes of the north, west, and south. They show some relationship to the belief systems of the Plains and Algonquian tribes for Coyote was a culture hero there as well. The Flathead traveled all around the Upper Spokane area. The concept that they flattened their babies' heads in cradleboards is a myth. In 1909, many were moved to Dayton Creek near Flathead Lake. The Flathead were neighbors of the Coeur d'Alene with Spokane to the west, the Kalispell to the north and the Pend d'Oreilles to the east, sharing borders with the Nez Perce. There are magnificent Ponderosa Pine trees all throughout this area. This one tree must have been magnificent to behold, or perhaps we are still living in it!

Names of the Salishan Tribes up by the Flathead

Lower Fraser Tribe = T'emsiu, Lamsiu'

Shuswap = Sihwe'pe ('people at the bottom)

Okanagon = Otcenake' (river people)

Sanpoil = N poi'lce or Snpoi'lexec (?)

Wenatchi = Snpeeskwa'use (place name)

Coeur d'Alene = Stci'tasui (?)

Nez Perce = Seha'pten (country area)

Umatilla = Kie'us (?)

Yakima = Ia'qima (?)

Dalles tribes = Senkaltu' (above the falls)

Shoshone = Sno'wa' (snake)

Lilooet = Snx'elami'ne or (ax people)

Conteau = Lu'keteme' (people of the slope)

Similkameen = name of the country

Colville = stone grainer for dressing hides

Columbia = Snakia'use (Cayuse)

Upper Kutenai = Ska'lsi (Kootenai River)

Walla-Walla = Sulawa (place name)

Paloos = Stekamtci'ni (mouth of snake)

Wasco = Watsqo'pe (falls)

Bannock = Axwe'elsa (bark covering)

Lemhi Shoshoni =T'C'etxwqoi' sten (mountain Snake)

General Name for Flathead People = Tcesntokain s Tke'lix = noon people or south people.

Skunk Children / Ottawa

The red sky lit up the evening as we walked along the river near Cochiti Pueblo. The older man held firmly to his cane with the three prongs hitting the terrain with conviction. "I am not from here, this is the way of the Pueblo people, when a man marries a woman he has to come and live with her family." Gregario shook his head, his white bangs danced on his forehead. "Then I had to make peace with my mother-in-law who called me Skunk!" He chuckled. "I was raised at the Mackinac Agency in Michigan with a whole bunch of other native kids. We didn't have a choice when they came out to where we were living and picked up my brother and me. My parents were told that if we didn't get on the bus, they would be taken to jail for life. We got on the bus, but we never saw our parents again."

Gregario stopped and pulled out his handkerchief and wiped his face. "My brother spent years searching for them, but they had been moved by the government. No one knew where they were or what had happened to them. The government changed peoples' names back then to names they could spell and pronounce. Those were hard times. I don't even remember my real name, just the name the teachers gave us." He pointed to a large flat lava rock with his cane. "Let's sit, my feet are tired."

"There was an old man from the Quapaw Agency on Indian Territory, he adopted me and told me the stories of the old ones. He told me the great story of true love and how the loss of love can bring shame to a man and his family. You ready to hear this?"

The Story of Skunk Children

There was a northern tribe of Ojibwa that lived further north, but on the same shore of Lake Michigan. This group was known as the Ottawa. After a very long and cold winter, a hunter's woman gave birth to a set of twins. Many of the Ottawa people believed that twins were a curse. The people around the lake stayed away from them.

In the fall when the babies were stronger, the Ottawa hunter and his wife decided that it would be best if they moved away from the main group to hunt for skins and find their own food. The hunter worried about her coming outside with him in the cold of winter to help with the trapping. The hunter usually went alone in the early mornings to place his traps all around the lake.

He would dig a hole in the ice, place his beaver trap, and move on to repeat this technique.

One morning, when he returned home to get more traps, he was met by his wife. She stood at the door with the two little babies bundled up in furs around her back. In her hands she held his traps. "I can come with you and help you as we have always done. The babies are sleeping and warm." The hunter frowned at her. "No, I don't want you out there, it is bitter cold. What if something should happen to you? What if you should fall in the ice?"

His woman shook her head. "I have never fallen in the ice. It is good for the babies to learn early how we live and how to exist in the frozen cold. I am coming." The hunter pulled the traps out of her hands. "No, I don't think you should." He turned and walked hurriedly ahead of her. The woman followed him for she was determined to be of help. As she walked in his steps, she passed one of his traps in the ice. Reaching down, she pulled up a beaver. "Husband, look a beaver! You must come and kill it!"

The husband trudged on ahead. He didn't turn back, but spoke over his shoulder, "If I kill that beaver the others might become frightened and escape from the ice through the trap holes. I will not kill it. You carry it up to higher ground and bind it to a tree."

His woman stood there, dangling the beaver on the end of the trap. "You would rather let it suffer than come right now and kill it? The other beaver will hear its suffering cries and then they will leave the area. Come now! Kill it now and I will take it back to the wigwam."

The hunter stopped. Slowly, he turned to look at her and the beaver. He was quite a distance away by now. "Woman, I will not walk all the way over there to kill that beaver that you found in the trap. You can let it go or you can take it up on the high ground and bind it. Do with the beaver as you wish." He continued to walk away from her.

The woman pulled the trap free. She let the beaver go. Quietly, she turned to go in the opposite direction. She walked all day and into the night. The babies slept.

That evening the hunter returned to the wigwam. There was no fire.

His woman was not there and the babies were gone. He thought that she had gone to visit a friend, maybe to show off the beaver she had caught. The hunter waited all night. His woman did not come home by first light. Searching for her, he found that she had traveled south for her prints were heavy with her burden of the babies. Following the prints, he saw that they changed shape. Her footprints were more and more like those of a large, heavy skunk. He followed her trail until it ended in a marshy place. This place is called Chi' c-ago. As he walked along, he saw skunks poke their heads out of the tall grass. There were skunks everywhere, little ones, big ones, baby ones, all peeking out through the grass watching him. The hunter sat among the skunks all day, calling his wife. A big skunk did get close to him, but then ran away. He couldn't kill them for fear that they were his family. After several days, the hunter returned to his people on the lake. The people after that referred to that area as Chi' cah-goh, or 'The Place of Skunks.' His father reminded him that it was a curse to be the father of twins.

The Ottawa were part of the northern Minnesota group or the Mide'wiwin or "Grand Medicine Society" of that tribe. The group falls under the linguistic name of Menomini and was titled as such in 1890 by Washington politicians. The earliest recording of this group was done in 1634, by a fellow called Nicollet. Their history is connected with the Winnebago of northwestern Wisconsin, and it is believed that at one time they occupied the same region. The Menomini had a tradition, similar to the Potawatomi Indians, of living at the edge of marshes. The marsh where they mostly stayed is where the city of Chicago is now situated. The people had such good hunting in that area, that they stayed. At night, their dogs would run to this one place and bark and bark all night.

This was known as the 'Place of Skunks,' and thus Chicago got its name. The term skunk in the Native language can refer also to a badger.

There were many groups of natives who felt that twins were a curse—either because they were twice as many mouths to feed or because one had done something to upset the spirits. At times, the only way a man and his woman would be able to stay with their people was if they placed the twins out in the wild to fend for themselves or perish. This belief was typical of early Western Civilization in Europe as well.

Totems of the Menomini

Kine'u - Golden Eagle

Pinash'iu - Bald Eagle

Opash'koshi - Turkey Buzzard

Kaka'ke - Crow

Piwat'inot - Beaver

Una'wanink- Pine Squirrel

Shawan'nani - Fork tailed Hawk

Opash' kushi - Turkey buzzard

Pakash'tsheke'u - Swift flying Hawk

Inaq'tek - Raven

Oamas'kos - Elk

Nama'uu' - Beaver near water or Skunk on land

Sons Of Sun Woman / Kiowa

Sunny and Cheri Davidson walked up the hill to the park. Their four year old son ran ahead to the swings. He jumped on one and began pumping his little legs until he was high in the air. Sunny hurled a gingham sheet into the air, spreading it out on the grass. "Here, we can sit here. Cheri brought us some snacks while she plays with him." He jutted his chin towards his son. "Grandma tells this story and she will be here directly." He smiled to open the brown paper bag. Potato chips, relish, hot dogs in buns, and tall jugs of water were placed on the sheet. The sound of an old pickup truck resonated through the air. "Ah, here she comes, Grandpa is bringing her."

The old woman was of an age that was beyond measuring. She was lifted from the back of the pickup truck by her two grandsons, one of whom was Sunny. Her woven green metal lawn chair was an extension of herself. She laughed, chortling in a language I did not understand. The food made her clap her hands. An old man equal to her in age or possibly older slid out of the driver's side of the truck. His legs were permanently bent with his arthritis. His hands were gnarled, decorated with scars and broken nails. Carefully, he followed his wife up the hill to the food on the sheet.

Once everyone was sitting on the sheet, the old ones began to notice me. Grandmother smiled and held out her hand. "Hey, hup." I touched her hand gently. Her smile grew wider. "You know the ways of the old ones?" I nodded. "Then let me share with you a story of the old ones. We are not from here, we arc not from here at all, we are just visiting this place and soon we shall go back to where we belong with the spirits." Her eyes closed, wrinkles moved and danced across her face as she spoke.

The Story of Sons Of Sun Woman

One bright and sunny day, a young girl was playing with her friends on the edge of a forested area. She noticed a porcupine in the branches of a tree. She raced ahead of her friends to grab the lower branches where she swung up into the tree to catch the porcupine. As she climbed the tree, it grew. The tree lifted her higher and higher into the sky. She looked down to see her friends yelling and screaming for her to climb down, but she could not, she was scared she would fall. The tree rose up into the sky and soon it pierced through the sky arch. The tree entered into the Upper World.

The porcupine, that had been above her now changed shape. He took on his proper form—the Son of the Sun. The young girl who had climbed the tree was no longer a small girl, but had grown into a beautiful fine young woman. The Son of Sun lifted her off the branch to place her in the Upper World. The young woman pulled away from him, for it was her people's custom that if a man were to look into a woman's eyes they were to be married. The young woman held firmly onto the tree branch near her. "I cannot be here, this is not the place of my people. It is important that you take me back for my family will be worried." The Son of Sun said nothing, he turned and walked away.

The young woman was from a strong Kiowa family. She climbed back onto the tree branch and stayed the night there. She did not complain. She just waited. Much time went by before the Son of Sun returned to her. He brought her food, a beautiful white robe, and a basket filled with different types of berries and nuts. Slowly she gave in to her need for food and ate. As she chewed her food, her memory of where she had come from and her family faded in her mind. When she was finished eating, she went with him as if it was the most natural custom. Son of Sun took her to his family and introduced her to his father and mother. There they were married.

It was not long after that she became heavy with child. Her condition made her hungry for a certain type of berry. She would go out alone in search of this berry and once finding the bush, she would eat all the berries that she could. Her hunger was such that it couldn't be satisfied. Finally, she decided to go out and find more berries. Her husband told her, "You must stay away from the azon bush. If the top of it has been eaten off by a buffalo you must move around it. Do not pick the fruit around it, do not go near it, for it will be bad."

The young woman now had this bush firmly in her mind. She walked to the people asking for the flowering bush. Those she asked knew better than to say anything. All day, she searched for this one bush. She found one! She found one that had been eaten by the buffalo. In the middle of the bush, where the buffalo had chewed, was a hole that went down all the way to earth. She stood there and looked down at the tall forests and the birds flying over the plains. Old memories came flooding back to her.

As she stood staring down, she gave birth to a fine baby boy. Suddenly, she grabbed the bush branches and wrapped them together into a rope. The young mother lowered herself and her baby down the rope. This was difficult for she was holding the baby with one hand and the rope with the other.

Her husband had returned from the hunt to find her gone. He was worried that she might have given birth alone. Calling out her name, he ran searching for her until he found the flowering bush. There he saw the rope moving down to the earth.

Looking down he saw his woman with the baby dangling from the end of the short rope. "What are you doing? Where are you going? This is your home!" He yelled down at her. "I need to return to the earth. The earth is my home not up there. My baby needs to know his family and his people. I cannot stay up there with you anymore!" She swung from the rope afraid to let go. Son of Sun let his anger overtake him. He picked up a large sharp rock and threw it, splitting her head wide open. She fell to the ground dead. The baby flew free to land on the soft leaves of a forest floor. He crawled to his mother's side where he suckled from her and hid inside of her.

The baby boy grew, but he was fearful of leaving his mother's body. Spider Woman crawled out of the forest to cautiously explore the sounds coming from the dead body just at the edge of the forest. There she found the small baby. Spider Woman spun a web of protection around the baby boy. Each morning and evening she brought him food from the forest. The baby boy learned to eat the mashed berries and nuts brought by his Grandmother Spider Woman. She taught him the language of the people there and showed him how to stand on his own two feet.

The boy learned to trust Spider Woman, who took him away from his mother's rotting carcass to wash him at the river. The boy learned how to hunt, to make hides for clothes, to find his own food, and to make a shelter for himself and his Grandmother Spider Woman. Grandmother Spider Woman taught him many stories of his people. She was preparing him to be a great man.

Early one morning, while Grandmother Spider Woman was busy weaving her web, the boy ran outside to play with his gaming wheel. Grandmother Spider Woman had shown him how to make it and was teaching him how to use it to ready him for competition with the other boys. The boy threw the gaming wheel high up into the sky, higher than the clouds. He stared up, trying to find it, when suddenly it came down and cut him in half. The boy stood there and stared. Beside him was another boy, just like him.

The boys raced back to Grandmother Spider Woman. She was prepared for this for she knew the ways of magic. Now she knew that these boys were not of the people, but had been sent to protect the people. She taught them how to kill beasts, monsters, and ghosts. Grandmother Spider Woman sent them out when they became young men to perform these tasks. They removed most of the destructive monsters from the earth. The two young men at times would travel in different directions, but if one was in trouble, the other knew it immediately and would come to his rescue.

After years of accomplishing amazing adventures and battles, one of the young men walked into a lake. He waved to his brother and disappeared beneath the waves never to be seen again. The surviving brother walked until he came to the Kiowa people. There he transformed himself into spiritual medicine called a'dalbedhya, or sometimes it is called "boy medicine" for it came from the magical boy who became a man. His spiritual medicine was divided up into ten pouches and was only allowed to be used by the most powerful of medicine men. Several small scalps are kept in the pouch with the medicine, and the pouch always has its own tipi.

"The Kiowa are not an agricultural people," the teller said when she had finished her story. "They are hunters. Grandfather told me this story that the Kiowa started up in the extreme North of the United States. They were driven south by wars. They moved quickly out of harm's way with the help of dogs pulling sledges.

"There is the story of the two chiefs who had a dispute over the possession of an udder from a female antelope, a delicacy. The Kiowa then divided up into two different groups.

"One Kiowa group moved to the southeast, crossed the Yellowstone and continued until they met with the Crows. There they settled for a time until they grew restless of the Platte River country and moved across the Republican and Smoky hills until they reached Arkansas. There the Kiowa took over much of the land in the Arkansas area.

"The other group of Kiowa went to the Northwest. When the Nez Perces were moved as prisoners to crude unfamiliar Indian Territory in 1883, many of them spoke the Kiowa language which they had learned from the Kiowa who lived in the 'white mountains' west of the old home of the Nez Perce in Idaho. Kiowa raided from Arkansas to Arizona, crisscrossing New Mexico and Texas, moving north into Canada, or into southeastern states. Kiowa petroglyphs have been found in New Mexico and Texas. Raiding horses and cattle, stealing women and children, hunting and trading maintained their subsistence.

The teller laughed,"The casinos now take back some of what is theirs! Hah!"

Creation Brothers / Kato-Pomo

A hard wet wind hit against the side of the vehicle as we parked on the lot. "You know where my people are from, right?" His face showed his eagerness to please. I quietly shook my head 'no.' His hands clenched in his lap. The teller is a tall fellow with a salt and pepper crew cut that accentuates his long square face. Piercing, dark brown eyes reflect his serious nature. His deep velvet voice is crisp, clear, almost as if he were giving a recital. His wife was sitting in the front of their red pickup truck reading a book whose cover was not visible.

He agreed to meet with me here at the rest stop between Socorro and Albuquerque. The snow fell softly like feathers to the ground as he unfolded his story. The warmth came from the story alone.

"We are from the territory of the Kulanapan family bounded by the Pacific Ocean and on the east by the Yukian and Copehan territories. On the north of the old land was the Russian River and on the south was Bodega Head. Father used to tell us of his visits to Santa Rosa and Sonoma County in California when he was just a small boy."

Dark clouds rolled in, "You said your daughter is in the Navy?"

We shared stories of boot camp and the trials of finding your right place in the Navy. Finally, he settled down enough to tell me the story he had been taught as a boy.

[Confirmed by the University of California Publication in American Archaeology and Ethnology, v, 184, No.2.]

The Story of Creation Brothers

*T*here were the two brothers, Nagai'tcho and Thunder. They walked about in the sky. They liked it there, but a sandstone rock which made the sky was very old and didn't have a purpose. Nagai'tcho and Thunder decided to stretch it. Thunder made his noise in the east, then again in the south, then the west, and in the north. Thunder was very loud and very powerful. The sandstone rock stretched each time it thundered until it was very wide and long. The two brothers tied down the corners.

Nagai'tcho walked on the sandstone. He walked to the south and stood on the large sandstone rock. He walked to the west and jumped on the rock, moving he walked to the north and pounded on the high round rock, then to the east where he patted the jagged rock. Nagai'tcho then made everything as it should be with canyons, hills, mountains, and the road for the sun to travel in each season.

Nagai'tcho and Thunder saw it was all very barren. They put trees in the south with some flowers. Nagai'tcho made a tiny hole in the north for the clouds to come through to bring rain for the trees and flowers. In the west, he put another hole for the clouds to return. These two had to think of everything themselves and they were very creative. Nagai'tcho made a long sharp knife by taking a stone and spitting on it, grinding it, and rubbing it.

While he was making the knife he thought about things. "This place is not ready yet. You go to the north and I will go to the south, let's stretch this place out some more." Nagai'tcho went to the north, untied it, and pulled it with all his strength. Thunder did the same at the south end. This they felt was good.

Nagai'tcho asked, "Where are you going to get the clouds once they are gone, how will they come back?"

Thunder pointed upland. "Make a fire here and the clouds will come." This is what they did and clouds came. They put the clouds high up above the sandstone place so Nagai'tcho wouldn't be bumping into them all the time.

Thunder has his own home way up high above the sandstone place. He said to Nagai'tcho, "I will continue to live up there, but you will be down here. What are you going to do down here with this place?"

Nagai'tcho smiled. "I will make myself some company. I will make animals and people out of the sandstone. I will make fire and the water." Nagai'tcho put water on the fire, around the edges there was dark mud. First, he made many animals, birds, insects and water animals. He decided to make people. First he made two legs, two arms, put grass for a person's belly and heart. He molded a round piece of clay for the man's liver and put lumps of mud for lungs. He pushed a hollow reed down the throat for breathing.

Fascinated, Thunder watched all of this, asking, "What are you going to use for blood? He has to have blood for that feeds his spirit."

Nagai'tcho took a piece of the ochre sandstone and pounded it into powder. "I will use the same blood as I did on the animals. Get me some of the water, Thunder." Thunder dribbled water on the powdered mixture, Nagai'tcho poured mixture all over the figure. "Hum," said Thunder, "what about his private parts? He'll need these if he is to be complete."

Nagai'tcho thought for a minute. "Let me have some more water for I need to make his eyes, mouth, nose, ears, and other things first. These will be more important than private parts." Thunder dropped more water. "Nothing I can think of would be more important to a person than their private parts, but that's just my opinion."

"Yes, it is just your opinion. They need to breathe, talk, eat and sleep, before they get into complications." Nagai'tcho worked hard on the face and even finished the hands and feet. Then he took a piece of clay and rolled it between his hands. He took this straight tube of clay and placed it between this figure's legs, right under the belly. "There, he has his parts."

Thunder laughed. "You aren't very creative. Those look like the animal's private parts. What will he do with them? He is alone!"

Shaking his head, Nagai'tcho gathered up more clay. They repeated the process, but this time he split this figure between the legs and with a stick gave this person a hole there. "Now, there is one of one kind and one of another just like the animals, insects and birds."

Thunder approved. "This is good, soon there will be many."

Clouds came through the sky hole. Rain fell on the land and fog covered the sandstone land with its trees and flowers. The sky became hot and damp. Thunder shivered at the unfortunate weather. "At least up where I am, the weather is pleasant, not like down here. How are these people going to see? It is dark down here all the time. They'll be bumping into each other and become cracked."

Sun came, warmed the land, and dried the damp. It was decided Sun would come up during the day to heat up the sandstone place and Moon be cold.

The two of them were feeling very powerful after doing all these things. Thunder came down from his high place. Pointing at a high cliff escarpment, Thunder dared Nagai'tcho, "Who do you think can split that rock the first time?" "Hah! I can," Nagai'tcho said, "do you think you can split that tree in half?" "Sure, I will do both." Thunder split the rock and cracked the tree in half within a blink. "Now it's your turn, Nagai'tcho." Nagai'tcho couldn't do either. Thunder strutted around in the sky, rumbling, "I am the most powerful! "

Nagai'tcho dared Thunder, "Who do you think can walk on water?"

Thunder rolled out in laughter. "Let me see you try first!"

Nagai'tcho stood on the water and sank. Thunder roared with delight as he stood on one leg and floated. Thunder roared and roared. Water fell on the sandstone land. It continued to fall as the two dared each other in one game after another.

Finally, Thunder gave the last dare, "Nagai'tcho, do you think you can jump up to the sky?"

Nagai'tcho was frustrated at losing every single attempt and answered, "Certainly, I am an excellent jumper!" He jumped and fell with a thud.

Thunder was having such great fun, he bellowed out as he leapt to the sky. Rain fell. Water covered everything. Nagai'tcho was so tired he didn't notice. These two were very careless.

While the rain fell, the water raised, frantically the animals tried to stay alive. People drowned for they were not as clever -they weren't the first made. Whale swam round and round in circles and became a woman. This is why women are always plump and when they work they go round and round. Some animals became sea lions at Usal and they are there today. At this time, the fish that existed were so frightened most died right away.

Blue lizard slid into the water and became a sucker. Bull snake slithered into the wet muck and once the water covered him, he became the black salmon. Salamander turned into a hook bill salmon. Grass snake became a steel head salmon. Tiger lizard became a trout. Trout was swimming frantically searching for his food when the others heard him, and they threw a net over him. But he became a clever trout and got away.

There was so much water for such a long time that abalones and mussels grew along the water. Kelp, of two kinds, was born in the water. All different kinds of water life came to be in this great flood. After a time, the foam on the water turned to salt. This was the way many life forms survived.

Sun came out after the clouds disappeared into the west. Sun dried up the mud.

Woman made a house. Out of this house came grizzly bear with his ferocious claws and teeth. Later, a male child appeared, coming out of the house. This is the belief that the woman, who came from a whale, brought birth to people with the help of the visiting bear and every since this men growl when they are hungry or angry.

Nagai'tcho awoke when the weather warmed. Thunder came back down when he heard the clouds leave. They looked around at the place they had made. "Some have lived, this is good."

Nagai'tcho made a dog from the mud. "This dog will be my friend and warn me when things are not right. He will wake me if something happens while I sleep. I shall keep him with me." Nagai'tcho placed high ridges between the land and the dwellings. "This will keep the ocean out. It will rise, but not overflow again."

"People will eat fish, big fish," Thunder whispered now, so as not to disturb the clouds. "Sea lions will be able to come ashore and the people can hunt and eat them. Devil fish are ugly, but they will taste good. There are so many fat fish floating around, the people will always have good tasting food."

Nagai'tcho smiled. "There will be water panther and stone fish that will attack people. Long tooth fish will kill the sea lion and live in the water. This will make things interesting. "

Thunder grinned. "Then sea lion will have no feet. I will give him a tail and large teeth. He won't have any trees in the ocean to hide behind and the ocean shall be powerful so he will have to be strong to survive."

Nagai'tcho placed tall redwood and fir trees along the ridges and the shore. He made them strong and tall. He placed pine tree forests up on the mountains for the people to have fuel and shelter. He put the yellow pines there, too, but not in the south.

Thunder placed stones to be natural dams. He dragged his foot to make creeks. "Here," he said, "this will run with water which has no salt and will be drinkable to the animals and people. Salt water tastes terrible and won't be good for them." Thunder found quiet dark places in the forests of tall trees where he kicked holes in the rich earth to have springs flow with clear, sparkling water. "This water is for the deer, birds, squirrels, and forest animals."

Near the springs, Nagai'tcho put oak, redwoods, firs, and more pines. They both decided acorns should grow from the oak to feed some animals. Deer became the animal that the people would eat. Grizzly bears would guard the deer. Panthers were placed in the mountains with the Grizzly bears to make sure the people wouldn't kill too many animals. Jack rabbits and all kinds of insects were placed on the mountains and on the flats.

Nagai'tcho smiled at his brother. "The people and animals will need places to hide, build homes, and birds to tell them of the seasons. Let's make lots and lots of birds!" Thunder laughed. "You make the birds of day and I will make the birds of the night. " The two brothers worked side by side for days building and making life forms. Bushes and brush were placed along the mountains for the animals to feed off of and to hide in from people and each other. Barking owls, screech owls, little owls, blue jays, grouse, quails, wood rats, robins, woodcocks, yellow hammers, sap suckers, mocking birds, meadowlarks, heron, black birds, turtle doves, pigeons, kingfishers, buzzards and ravens, chicken hawks, robins, were placed to warn and befriend the animals on the ground.

Thunder talked to the clouds and told them to feed the streams which ran into the valleys, so the people and animals would always have fresh water. Chestnuts, hazelnuts, manzanita berries, buckeyes, pepper nuts, grasses, and bear clover grew for the animals and birds to share.

Nagai'tcho said to his dog, "Things are good. This is a beautiful place. Everything is growing and everyone has something to eat." Thunder called to his brother, "Nagai'tcho, it is time for us to leave each other. You have made a good place here for the people and animals, but it is time for me to go up into the sky and make my own family. I would ask you to visit, but you can't jump high enough! Hah, hah, ha!"

Nagai'tcho scratched his dog behind the ears. "Thunder brother, have a good life. I hope you have many little thunder clouds. My dog and I will find our place here. My children are these people and they will need all my help to survive. We are going up into the mountains, near the spring water. I will go home." Nagai'tcho went to the north. His dog is still there, watching, ready to give warning if something were to happen. Everything is in its place. The brothers worked well together. We thank them.

The teller pulled out an old yellowed paper with a map on it. He pointed to the west coast. "The Pomo are known as the "Lake People." They lived on the west coast of California. The First People were located in the valley between the South Fork of Eel River, the Main River and on the headwaters of the South Fork, extending in a narrow strip to the Pacific Ocean." Very slowly he wrote out in pencil on the back of his black notebook all the Tribes. Each name flowed from his hand, as he called them out by rote.

Different Tribes of the Kulanapan Family

Ballo Kai Pomo = Oat Valley People

Batemdika'yi

Buldam Pomo = Rio Grande or Big River people

Chawishek

Choam Chadila Pomo (Capello)

Chwachamaj'u

Dapishul Pomo (Redwood Canyon)

Eri'o (mouth of Russian River people)

Gallinomero (Russian River below Dry Creek)

Kabinapek (western Clear Lake Basin)

Kai Pomo (Eel River and South Fork people)

Koma'cho (Anderson and Rancheria Valleys)

Kulanapo

Misalamagun or Musakakun (north of Healdsburgh)

Senel (Russian River Valley)

Siako (Russian River Valley)

Yokaya Pomo (Lower Valley People)

Eastern People (Clear Lake about Lakeport)

Eru'ssi (Fort Russ area)

Guala'la (Northwest corner of Sonoma)

Kaime' (above Healdsburgh)

Kato Pomo (Lake People)

Kula Kai Pomo (Sherwood Valley)

Lama (Russian River Valley)

Poam Pomo

Shodo Kai Pomo (Coyote Clan)

Sokoa (Russian River Valley)

Yus'al Pomo (Ocean People)

Spirit Children / Keres

Some say this story comes from the northern area of New Mexico, but my teller told me that for a fact this story came from the central area of New Mexico. "We don't have people this strange up north, aside from the Hippies and the politicians." Tommy Roanhorse let out a truck driver's laugh. "Hah, had you fooled, didn't I?"

I smiled at him. "Well, I am from Espanola and I know that we don't have people like this up there!"

He shook his head. "Shame on you. Espanola is your town? No wonder you are collecting stories. There aren't any good ones in Espanola, only really bad jokes!" He slapped his hand on his dirty, dusty, leather chaps. "Heck, I know people in Espanola and this story is from further south." He rubbed his parched lips with the back of his hand. "All right, you want a story from the old ones, stand back, because here it comes!"

The Story of Spirit Children

They were the two who sat alone. A woman and a man, both of age to be married, both stayed alone. Those two sat alone. The young woman was the daughter of a great hunter who disappeared during one very cold winter. Her father had been searching for food and never returned. The girl grew into a woman and no one wanted to be with her because she didn't have anything of value.

Another hunter had found the baby boy out on the plains in summer. The baby was alone, there was no one with him. He was hungry, shaking, and needed care. The man brought him home to his family. The woman of this man would have nothing to do with the baby boy. She had children to care for those of her own blood. She didn't need anyone else's baby. Her man gave the baby boy to his grandparents who raised this boy to be a strong man, but the young man did nothing but sit and think. He would not hunt or fight. He ate his share, helped grandmother with firewood, and then he would sit and think. That was all he did.

The girl, who was now a woman admired this young man. She would finish her chores only to go sit by him. She would sit with him and say nothing, just watch him thinking. At times he would sing a song. She would accompany him. Other times he would chant and she would thump a stick to keep time. Rarely did they speak to one another. They mostly sat. They spent most of the day together.

People in the village left them alone. They had important tasks to accomplish. The men were hunting in the North and the women were grinding corn or collecting yucca root for winter. The grandparents were teaching and training the little ones on the important aspects of life. Young men were learning healing chants, young women were learning how to skin and cure meat. The villagers were not to be bothered with these two young people who sat and thought all the day.

Winter storms brought a harsh wind from the north. Scouts returned to the village warning of snow storms. The women were ready. They rolled up the summer skins, attached them to travois (long poles bound together with leather straps, making a carrying basket) to the horses and dogs. Babies were strapped in cradle boards, small toddlers were wrapped in blankets to be belted to travois. The grandmothers had the dried food wrapped and placed in baskets, the older children raced after the dogs to harness them, and the grandfathers prepared the bows, arrows, spears, and leather wrist wraps for later. Everyone was out of the summer village to move at a fast pace south back to the safety of the Pueblo for the winter.

Everyone was gone, except the two who sat on the rock and thought.

As the sun went down, the young woman hurried down the trail to the summer village. It was empty. There was no one. They were alone. He called to her, but she was walking, following the trail of horse hooves which went to the west. He ran to her and stopped her. "Don't go that way that is the way they planned for an enemy to follow. The people have wiped their tracks. We will not find them now." She frowned and shook her head, holding back the tears. "They left us here, they forgot us."

She stared up at him. "Do you know the way back to the Pueblo?"

He frowned. "No, I always followed everybody else. I never needed to know, Grandmother always took care of me. She told me what to do, I just followed the others."

Looking across the plain up to the mountain she choked on her tears. "Why would they leave? How could they leave us behind?" Shaking her head, she fell into his arms.

He led her up the mountain. "This is not good, there must be a snow storm coming or perhaps an attack, we should not be here. Come, we must move into the trees." The two of them hurried up into the dense forest. She wanted to build a fire, but he firmly told her, "No, we need to make a strong shelter first, something that will keep out the cold wind and the heavy snows. Right now we need to get to work." That night they had a temporary shelter from the strong gale-like winds. In the dark, she quietly dug dirt troughs for beds which protected them from the strong gale like winds. She softly began to cry, he quietly comforted her. Suddenly it was as quiet as it had been loud. He pulled her close to him. She sank into his hold. They were totally alone.

Time moved forward with the coming of the spring rains with thunder. The young man was now a full grown man. He built them a strong mud house with a smoke hole and a firm stone fire grate. She skinned the deer that he had killed and they ate well. There was plenty of dried jerky meat, plenty of chamisa wheat, berries and nuts in baskets by the door. Her man had a good supply of wood and food with the anticipation of the coming baby.

Spring came with crisp mornings and fine song birds. She gave birth to their first child and then over time with twins and triplets -soon they had twelve children. Each time she became heavy with child, he cared for her diligently. He did her chores, his chores, cared for the little ones, chopped wood, while showing the older ones how to care for those younger. But something was not right.

The children were neither male nor female. They were called H'lah'mon, someone who is both male and female. The father did not know who should be taking on the woman's duties or who should be learning the man's duties. The boys only looked like males because of their stature, but they had both female and male parts. Some were eager to clean and bake, while others were anxious to hunt then braid the little one's hair. All the children were firm and muscular, yet they had dim colored welts on their faces. Some had male parts that did not work; others had a female shape, but were stronger than others. The father was not sure what to do with his children. Their mother felt that her children were simple in the head. She would give them directions to do something, but they would forget what she had told them to do.

The older children would attack the younger ones for no reason. The younger children grew differently from the others. Some had long arms and long legs, but could not stand upright. Others had hard bony growths in their hair that itched. Many of the children refused to wear their clothes or take baths. The mother and father were at a loss as to how to raise these children. Their family lived in a home of chaos.

One night late, the mother and father went up onto the hill overlooking the valley to quietly have ceremony. They hadn't done one since the people left and were sure this was the cause of their problems. The father built a huge fire while the mother sprinkled corn meal, chanting to the spirits. The father asked the spirits for guidance. "Who are these children that we have born? What are we to do with them to respect you? What is their purpose here?" The mother held her arms up to the night sky. "We need your guidance, with respect, help us."

As the sun rose in the early morning, both the parents were asleep near the dying fire. The father was given a dream by a spirit who told him, "Your children are to have names not of people, but of spirits. First, your oldest son is Pekwina, the Priest-Speaker of the Sun. He is a thoughtful one, even in the heat of the day, he will tell others when it is time to prepare for seasons.

"Your Second child is called Pi 'hlan Shiwani, for this one holds the knowledge of the Bow-Priest Warrior. This one is the spirit of the trees and shall be frightened by the least flutter of a leaf. Listen to this one and you will be protected. The Third child should be named Eshotsi which is the night bat of the forest. He can see better than anyone in the bright sunlight or in the darkest of nights. This one's visions will guide people to safety out in the open or in the mountains. Although he is good at tripping over his own shadow, he will be a good guide. The Fourth child is named Mauiyapona the Wearer of Eyelets of Invisibility. This one has horns like a catfish on his head and knobs on his body like a squash. He will frighten others and try to hide his head, but his body will scare those of danger away. The Fifth child's name is Potsoki the Pouter. This one will do little else but laugh and look bland. He will try to hide, but his laughter will help you find him. Potsoki is the spirit of joy and will bring light into the world.

"Your children born three at a time, are to be called in order: Na'hlashi the Aged Buck who is the biggest of them all. He shall be the Big One who can help you carry and build, but he will always be sad for being so big and will have fits of crying. Frisky as a Fawn will giggle like a girl, but never work. This one will prefer the world of magic and mind-made spirits, and will have great stories to tell and share. Carried Off, who is small, will be taken away from you by a snail to the underworld where Carried Off will have great purpose.

"Itseposa the Glum will mourn for the loss of the Carried Off child and will cry until Itseposa's eyes and lips are raw and chapped. After a time, this one will become happy again and be of much help to you and your wife. K'ya'lutsi the Suckling, and his twin Tsa'hlashi, the Old Youth, will teach the others of ceremony, tradition, and healing. These last two you must nurture carefully and be watchful of them. They will advise the others like priests, but they will grow old quickly, they will become too old to remember ever being young."

The father was awakened by his woman shaking him. "We best get back to the children. They will be hungry and doing who knows what? Come, we must go, hurry." The father explained his dream. She listened and smiled. "I had a similar dream. Each of our children is very special and will share something with the earth and the people who meet them. They are normal for themselves, we need to understand them."

After four winters, the villagers returned. They were surprised to find the two with a family. The children had become great priests, for they each had different spirit strength. They taught the people many lessons and rules of life that were to be obeyed or consequences would follow that could not be healed or corrected. The twins were taken by the spirits early for they were needed. The villagers learned to listen and accept that which was different from them, for in difference there is great wisdom. Each person's spirit has a specific purpose.

Keres refers more to a language than to a particular group. Tommy Roanhorse told me he was from Zuni Pueblo area. The Zuni do speak Keres, but refer to themselves as Shi-wi or 'the people.' They live in the southwestern part of New Mexico, but at one time were in both New Mexico and southeastern Arizona. The Keres language is part of the six southern Pueblo groups in New Mexico.

Deformed babies were considered to be very spiritual. There was nothing wrong with them for they held the Spiritual Powers of the being who helped form them. Each special baby was thought to be able to communicate with the Spirit World for they knew more than those of us who were born appearing to be "normal." The Spiritual children and adults were carefully cared for and watched in that they held secrets that the others needed to learn. This was a tender way to raise those who were "different." Today, doctors and social workers make a point of telling everyone how "handicapped" the Spiritual Ones are, yet they hold much more power than the doctors or social workers. Wonder who will tell them about this?

Tsityostinako and the Daughters / Tsia

The teller of this story moved to Albuquerque to be closer to work. He returns to his family for feast days and ceremonies, but finds it difficult to make a living there. His reason for telling this story was, "People should never forget the kindness of the Sacred Sisters before they began to compete."

The Story of Tsityostinako and the Daughters

In the first time there was only Tsityostinako and her daughters, Utctsiti and Naotsiti. Fog and clouds filled the whole of the world, for that was all there was. Tsityostinako decided to make the four worlds.

The beginning world at the bottom was Yellow. Above it was the Blue-green world and above that world was the Red world. At the top of all of these was the White world. Tsityostinako and her daughters started out in the Yellow world. Utctsiti and Naotsiti had a thick manta, a blanket that women wore, which they placed flat on the ground. Utctsiti created the cacique (census taker) first for she needed him to take care of the people and love them as a mother loves her own children.

Tsityostinako took her daughters to the ceremonial house to place the manta on sacred ground. They placed a medicinal cane on top of the manta and chanted. People of different purpose were taken out from under the manta. It was decided that Tsityostinako was terrifying all the people who came out from under the manta and she should stay hidden. The daughters would pick up the manta and see who they created while gingerly taking them outside to name. Tsityostinako put ideas into Naotsiti's head as to who should have what role.

After they created the iariko or ear of corn fetish, in a form of a woman, Utctsiti told her what her work would be and how she was to watch and care for the earth and the people running free. When iariko heard of her duties, she cried. There was much for her to do, but she would do her best. The sisters created all the sacred clan societies. Each one was named, given a purpose, and set outside to join the others.

Shakanyi was created and then the Koshaire who was to be the guide over the songs and rituals.

Next was the creation of the animals. All were made in pairs, female and male. There were special animals that had to be taken far from the others, such as the lion, bear, badger, wolf, eagle, and shrew. These were to help the yaya (mothers and medicine men). The daughters created a Blue Spruce and planted it for the people to climb to the next world. They sang songs to get it to grow faster. The Koshairi went first, then Tsityostinako and her two daughters and all the societies and the people in the order in which they had been created. Everyone made it to the Blue-green world.

The people were fed magically by the sacred sisters. They stayed there for four years. The sisters then made a henati or cloud tree and planted it. It grew up to the Red world. Koshairi was called to try out the tree and he climbed it to the Red World. He thought it was fine. The people stayed in the Blue-green world for four years. Then everyone ascended to the Red world. They stayed in the Red world for four years. Here the people learned of ceremonies, medicine, and traditions. The sisters made a heyoc or type of fog tree. They sang and it grew. Koshairi was told to try out the tree and he did, he climbed it up to find solid rock.

The sisters sent Badger to climb the tree. He dug for a time until he came to a rock. Badger came down and told them the rock was open, but there were sharp sides to it and someone could get cut. The sisters sent up a cicada that made his noise and smoothed out the edges to the White world. Everyone started climbing the tree. The people were thankful and the yaya thanked the sisters for leading the way. Some fell back down. They were the Wikori and the Hododo, the fathers of the Kwiriana. No one had missed them. When the Hododo and the Wikori reached the White world, you could hear them yelling and throwing rocks down to the worlds below. They came up with their deer horns. The sisters asked them why they had fallen behind and they had no answer. The sisters decided that they would be the ones who would be hunted. Once they were shot, the hunters would give thanks for their spirit and they would rise again. The home of the Hododo and the Wikori is in the northeast part of Tsia.

When the people settled, they built houses. The men were told to look for land where they could grow wheat, beans, melons and other crops. When each man had land, Utctsiti began to create seeds of all kinds for them to plant. She worked with the manta and created all kinds of game animals. Naotsiti began to create things more wonderful than her sister. Naotsiti created paper and it could talk to her and to her people. Utctsiti could not talk to paper and it would not talk to her. She felt angry about this and began to cry. Tsityostinako whispered into Utctsiti's ear and told her what the paper said.

The sisters decided to have contests to see which one had the greatest power. One would create something and challenge the other to guess what it was. One of Naotsiti's creations was a cross. Utctsiti challenged her sister to tell which way a bird was going by looking at the tracks. Natositi made soldiers to come and shoot at the Utctsisi's people. Utctsiti shot at the soldiers with her lightning and killed them all. At the end of the competition Naotsiti decided to run away. Tsityostinako appeared to be protecting Utctsiti and Naotsiti had no chance of winning. Utctsiti ran after her sister and caught her by the arm. Naotsiti pulled away, saying, "I will not fight against you anymore." Naotsiti turned into a wood rat and disappeared through a hole. Utctsiti was left to take care of life here in this place by herself.

The Animals the Sisters Created

Utctsiti	Naotsiti
Tsini - curly haired dog	De' - Coyote, called poseqwase'dndyo
(Small dog used in primitive times)	(These coyotes stole food)
K'u'jo - Gray Wolf of Isleta	Mu'jo - Red Fox, called de'tsa'ywe'i
K'ae'ntsa - white mountain lion, wild cat.	Musa - pueblo cat or raccoon
K'ae'n - Rocky Mountain Pima or Cougar	Kae'n - Lion of the wild mountains
Mat'fu' - big eared animal	N'wi'fsae'ii - white rat
Ob'I - wild duck	K'a'gi'- Canada Goose
P'I'ndi' - mountain turkey chicken	Di' - pueblo chicken
Ko':"nwi' - Western mourning dove	'Oka'wae - Turkey Vulture
Qwae'ypi" - Western Redtail	Tse' - eagle
Mahu'nn- owl	Ogo'w'I - road-runner
Kwae'ae - magpie	Se'eh - Pinion Blue Jay
'O'do' - Crow	Kah'ka-we' - Raven
Ko'ro'hi"y - horned lizard	Kod'u'u - Sonora skink
Po'paen'u - water snake	Usidi' - long snake, earth color
Piy'pah - flat-chested fish	Pa'e' - little fish, minnows
Polamimi- butterfly	Nee-nee pol'e - bright butterfly
F'u'uy' - cricket or locust	K'owi'ln- brown spit grasshopper
P'e' - black headed head lice	P'u'p'e - rabbit brush head lice
a>'wae'p'e - spider with web	'a'wae - tooth spider
O'ku - turtle or tortoise	Po'qwa' - salamanders
Ku'pi - red stone	A'anuk'eh - young girl
E'nu'keh - young boy	A'nu'h - girl in adolescence
E'nu'h - boy in adolescence	Kwi'h - woman in prime of life
Se'hn - man in prime of life	Kwi'jo - old woman

Se'ndo'h - old man

To'wa - human beings

Tsi's'oyo - big eyes

Hae'pa'n - large animals

Ku'nni-t'ainin = Goose Clan

Ke'h - Bear

Hododo and Wikori - fathers of Kwiraina

Leading Brothers / Chickasaw

The stories of the old ones are mostly about sadness and the relocation to the Indian Reserves, but on one afternoon as the rain was falling outside Walgreens on Rio Bravo there was an old man selling his ink drawings. His long hair was braided and his hands were carefully wrapping his drawings. One was of a bear in a cave with a child who had spots on his body. When the man was asked about the drawing he answered, "In the winter of 1830-40, the Chickasaw people were pushed west into the Kiowa and Comanche. It was thought the Chickasaw were running from the people of spots that came into their camp and left the spots behind to take away all the children and weak ones in the spring of 1838. It moved west and hit New Mexico in the spring of 1840 and was carried east again by the Santa Fe traders."

He lifted up another drawing of young people running on a flat plain with long sticks in their hands. His voice roared with laughter as he explained, "Good times we played with allied tribes such as the Chactas and Dakota on the upper Missouri in the ball field. The game was made up of women playing against the men, five of the women matched against one of the men. A mixed game of this kind was very amusing to watch.

"The Dakota women were allowed to play for they were great at winning. Women in other tribes were not allowed to touch a ball stick for it was considered unclean. How this works is a player offers a wager of some type of clothing, a robe, or a blanket and when an opponent lays down an object of equal value the game begins. The area of land is decided and two stakes are placed one on each side. There are two or three innings deciding on the number of players. The ball is tossed into the air in the center of the field. As soon as it comes down it is caught with a ball stick by one of the players and he sends it full speed in the direction of one of his own, who takes it up and races toward the stake.

"The player is to try and take the ball by striking the handle of the other players' to dislodge the ball. This is a difficult matter for the horizontal motion of the ball stick is moving quickly in the hands of the player. Sometimes the ball carrier is hit on the body and this disables him, especially if he is hit hard on the leg or arm which can be broken by the sticks. There are severe injuries when playing for high stakes like a horse or a woman.

"If the ball carrier on one side reaches the opposite goal, he needed to throw the ball to the other post. There is always a difficult matter for the ball can be misdirected if it hit another ball stick. The game may come to a close at the end of any inning by mutual agreement of the players, that side winning the greater number of scores is declared the victor by the team captains. We used to call this game 'baggataway.'"

I helped him carry his drawings, now wrapped in white paper to his truck and then asked him if he would like a cup of coffee at the Chinese Buffet. As we sat on the plastic chairs, he decided to tell me the First Story. Here is his version.

The Story of Leading Brothers

*T*his is the story of how the Indian people came to this country. Their first home was somewhere on the continent of Asia, but they were tired of living there and wanted to go somewhere else where they could live in a place without volcanoes and eruptions. The two brothers wanted to have a land of their own for their own people. They called everyone together to have a council meeting to decide how they might be able to move somewhere else. It was then that the trials and hardships began for them.

The two brothers asked the Creator for guidance and in a dream it was revealed that they must move forward, quickly. They were told to move east, so they set out in that direction. They had a dog whose duty was to guard the camp every night and he was used to keep the wild animals from attacking the people. During the night, as the people moved stealthily to the east, the dog was their guide. The name of the dog was Pan'ti. The dog took care of everything for most of the trip, for he didn't stop, he urged them forward.

If someone were to become ill, the people would stop for a time, do their magic cures, get the person well and move on again. If anyone was bitten by a snake, the dog would lick the wound and immediately the person would be cured. The people continued on for many days, many times of the full moon, on across the land to the east. Babies were born, some died, and even a few became lost and were never found.

Finally, they came to a large abyss filled with water. This body of water was called Ok'hata Lcto or Big Ocean. The people could go no further, the water completely blocked them. The dog whined, dug about on the beach, and howled, but the waters did not disappear nor did they break for the people to pass. At night they could see fires on the other side of the water, but their voices were not heard. It was agreed that a council should meet and decide what they should do next.

It was noticed by two young men that the waters ebbed at certain times of the day. This would allow for the people to build a raft which could go out with the waters at that particular time, causing them to cross the waters naturally. At last they crossed the waters and arrived in North America safely. There were some who did not make it, they fell overboard and drowned. It was very cold where they landed, many perished from the freezing weather, the cold ground that was white, and the lack of food.

There were the two brothers who called a council. Some requested an immediate departure from this area, while others were terrified of what might be beyond this land.

The people divided into two groups; those who wished to migrate to a warmer place with Pan'ti, for they loved him dearly, and those who were frightened and did not want to take risks, choosing to stay where they were. After a time the weather warmed. Those that moved to the east went forward cautiously for there were all kinds of poisonous snakes. If anyone did get bitten they had the dog to help with the wound. Winds blew across the open lands, sending the people up into the mountains of Montana. The people were able to hunt for deer, prairie chickens, turkeys, squirrels, fish and some moving creatures with horns. There were dangerous animals that hunted them such as the panther and wolf.

Pan'ti helped each one of the brothers' groups by killing numerous wild animals, while he drove the rest away. Pan'ti would bark at danger, howl when someone was lost, and pant when he knew the people were following him on the right path. The flat lands of Montana were not kind to the people. Pan'ti knew that soon it would be time to lead them further on their journey. Food became scarce in the early summer and it was decided to move again. The women remembered how hungry everyone was before when they traveled. Now they planned several days before leaving a campsite, to bake up breadstuffs like blue or shuck bread and cold flour flat bread. This food would be wrapped in blankets and carried on their backs. The people moved on with their trusty dog.

Cold winds pushed the people south. Pan'ti led them to the east, as he had been told to do by the Creator. After many days of traveling, they came to a mighty river that roared over the rolling earth. This they learned was called the Mississippi River. Here they camped for a time, uncertain as to how they could get to the other side. Finally, it was decided to construct another raft, similar to the first. The river was too strong for the raft. It ripped it to pieces; people were plunged into the cold mighty river. The stronger ones made it back to shore, pulled up by their families and friends. Dark clouds rolled overhead, when the people realized that Pan'ti had been taken by the river. He was gone!

This was all very sad. They didn't know what to do. In the night, one of the brothers had a dream in which the Creator told him to rise in the morning, go to the west, and there would be a sacred pole that would guide the people to the other side safely. The kohta wooden pole became their guide. Every night, when they would stop, the pole would be plunged into the earth. In the morning, the kohta pole would lean in a certain direction, this was the direction the people were to travel.

Kohta wooden pole was followed until they came to the Tennessee River. That night the pole was stuck into the ground, but in the morning the pole did not lean. It stood straight up, not moving one way or another. It was here that the people called a council. The two brothers came together, for they were now the oldest of the leaders, to talk to their groups. The oldest brother called out to them, "This is the place where we are to stay. We shall go no further for we are tired. The Creator has declared that this is the land of our people and it is here that we shall stay." He picked up the pole and thrust it with all his might into the wet ground. The pole stuck, straight.

The younger brother shook his head. "This is not our place. We were told to move to the east. Pan'ti gave his life leading us to the east. We cannot go against the wishes of the Creator, we must go east to the rising sun."

It was here that the groups divided. One group became the Chickasaw, the other remained to become the Choctaw. The two brothers ended up fighting the Creek Indians for land in brutal wars. The Chickasaw and Choctaw, one on each side of the river were about 100 in number, the Creek were 2,000 strong. As the grandfathers tell the story, two dogs, one white and one yellow, magically came to their rescue. The dogs were not visible to the Choctaw or Chickasaw, but the enemy could see them. The Chickasaw heard the dogs barking. Following the sound of the barking, they came upon the hidden Creek Indians.

The dogs were vicious and ripped the enemy right off their horses before they could harm the people of the brothers. Even later, when the brothers had to fight the French, they did so independently of the other group. This is the way of brothers, they must each go their own way. It was said that at night, one could hear Pan'ti howl when the rivers flooded. Some say he fell into squall and someday he will dig his way out to return to the people. Today the Choctaw will tell you that Pan'ti means 'cat tail,' but you don't have to believe them.

The Chickasaw are part of the Muskhoean tribes, living well beyond the Mississippi River. They also have a story telling of how people came from under the earth through a cave in the Mississippi-Nachee Indian country. This cave was shut after the two brothers realized people would not move forward as long as they could return to the cave. There is confusion regarding tribal affiliations.

"The Chickasaw in the past have represented the Kasihta Indian and claim them to be an offshoot of themselves, while the Kasihta say the Chickasaw was one of the original tribes from which the Creeks descended and associate them with the three tribes that are known today as Creek Indians of the Southeast." [Bureau of American Ethnology, 19th edition, 1897]

The tribe of Mushogean stock known as Chickasaw occupied northern Mississippi and adjacent areas of Alabama and Tennessee. The main tribe they befriended was the Chokchuma. The Chickasaw language was a dialect of Choctaw, although the two tribes were enemies and differ in character. The Chickasaw were nomadic and warlike while the Choctaw were famous for camping for a year or two when there was good hunting.

The teller of the above story explained that the Chickasaw settled in an area near Kingsport, Tennessee, south of the Blue Ridge and southwest to a point not far from present Atlanta. Throughout the colonial period in the United States, the Chickasaw were enemies of the French and friends of the English, but remained neutral in the American Revolution.

"The Treaty of Pontotoc in 1832 had them sell their lands east of the Mississippi and removed them to Indian Territory where they organized as the Chickasaw Nation. In 1890, the population of the Chickasaw Nation consisted of 3, 941 souls that were full blood and mixed bloods of the Chickasaw were 681." [1897, Bureau of Indian Reserve Statistics]

Brother Friends / Menominee

The storyteller grandmother wanted to explain right away where the name of her people came from and why the name is used in the Green Bay area of the United States.

"Menominee, the name Men-o-mine-e comes from Oma'nomiene'u ina'neu. Oma'nomi meaning 'rice' and ina'neu means 'man.' The Algonquin term for grain is Zizan'ia a'quat'ica which in English means 'wild rice born from water.' The French called the Menominee 'Fol Avoin' or Wild Oats. The Menominee lived around the whole of Green Bay area, covering some eight thousand square miles. The western boundary was the Mississippi River. The Winnebago, who were friends with the Menominee, lived on some of this land under agreed upon treaties."

The woman who met with me had her great grandmother's diary. The diary was written while her great grandmother was in a mission school on the Indian Reserve in the late 1800s. The young woman showed me her great grandmother's entry regarding the village doctor or Mashkikikewinini. The village doctor had been jailed for giving herbs to the sick. The writing told of her concern for the white doctor practiced medicine without consult and many times was wrong and the patient died.

At her village when a person became ill there was a consultation held with four medicine men and once the illness had been discussed, the ceremony was decided. Rarely did anyone die.

The diary held the hen scratches of the great grandmother remembering the story of the beginning. The young woman read it to me as the wind blew gently in the trees over our heads.

The Story of Brother Friends

The daughter of Noko'mis (Earth Mother) is the Mother of Ma'nabush, who is Fire. Flint was the first born of Noko'mis and lived here alone: Flint decided to make a bowl. He pushed the bowl into the earth and lifted up the dirt in the bowl. As Flint sang, the dirt in the bowl became blood. The blood grew and changed into a form. The blood became Wab 'us, the Great Rabbit. Flint sang slowly over the bowl, and then suddenly the Great Rabbit Ma'nabush hopped out of the bowl and became a man.

Ma'nabush thought he was alone. He had hopped far from Flint and was having a time of it for those who dwelt under the earth were shaking the earth, pushing up water, and trying to get at him. Ma'nabush decided to take up a piece of flint and make an ax. This he could use to strike the ana'maqki'yu (under the earth dwellers) who were trying to get at him from under the earth. Ma'nabush rubbed the flint against a rock. He put his mind into making the flint sharp. His rubbing went ke, ke, ke ka, ke ka, ke ka, goss, gosss, gosss. He sat back rubbing his hands. This rock told him he was alone. There was no mother, no father, no brother, no sister for him to call family. He was alone.

In the silence of his own thoughts he heard something come close to him. Ma'nabush turned quickly and there not far from him stood Moqai'o Wolf. Moqai'o Wolf put his head down and said to Ma'nabush, "I am your brother. We shall live as a family and I shall hunt for you."

Ma'nabush nodded to Moqai'o Wolf. "It is good to have a brother. You will no longer be a wolf, but a man." Moqai'o stood and was a man. Ma'nabush and Moqai'o moved to the shore of a large lake. There they built a wigwam. Each day, Moqai'o would hunt for food. One night, there was a heavy snow storm and the lake glistened with ice. Ma'nabush warned Moqai'o not to cross the lake for water was the power of the ana'maqki'yu. Night came quickly that day. Moqai'o felt that he would be safe if he hurried across the lake. He was only half way across when he was taken by the ana'maqki'yu. Ma'nabush knew Moqai'o was gone the minute it happened.

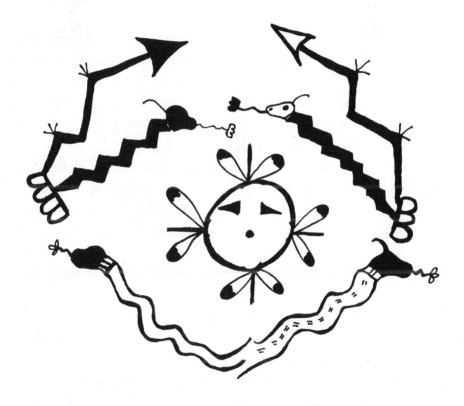

When Ma'nabush realized he had lost his brother, he went out of the wigwam and found many other people who said they were his uncles and aunts. They were the children of Noko'mis. Ma'nabush saw that they were being shaken and water was pushing up into their newly made wigwams by the ana'maqki'yu. The water kept coming and soon the people would drown.

Ma'nabush cried out for Noko'mis to help. He called out four times and the water began to disappear. All that was left was mud and sand. The chief of the ana'maqki'yu stood on what was once an island in the lake. Ma'nabush spoke to Mi'sikine'bik, the Great Fish. "I want to take your spirit for you have not allowed my people to drink water, and instead you choose to drown them." The smaller ana'maqki'yu heard this and split the earth, letting the waters from below fill the lake. The Great Fish jumped into the waters and was gone.

Ma'nabush went into the forest and cut down some trees with his sharp flint. He built himself a canoe. He was determined to take the spirit of the Great Fish by attacking it in the water. As he left the shore he sang out, "Great Fish, come and swallow me. Then I shall be yours." The Great Fish ignored Ma'nabush. The Great Fish is still alive, still trying to steal people from the earth like he did the brother of Ma'nabush.

One time after a long journey Ma'nabush thought he heard some singing and thinking there were people having a celebration he went to find them. He saw the head feathers moving in every direction but it was evening and he couldn't tell who was dancing. He waited for someone to invite him to the celebration, but no one appeared to notice him at all. Ma'nabush was a friendly person and he called out, "My friends, I have come to join you in this dance," as he was speaking someone behind him started laughing loudly. The same voice said, "We have fooled the great Ma'nabush!"

Ma'nabush looked around him and saw the ana'maqki'u, the tall reeds with feathery plumes of the swamp. This made him angry. "I will remember this and you will not be pleased." He left that place and walked for a long time to the sounds of music and dancing. As he got closer he could see that he was to be tricked again for these were many birds, of many kinds, dancing round and round in a circle.

Ma'nabush said to them, "My friends, I have some songs to sing for you while you dance, but you must keep your eyes closed as you dance, or you will not appreciate the sound of my voice." The birds began to dance and soon they were moving closer and closer to him. He grabbed four of the birds and wrenched their necks, pulling their heads off. He did this until he came to a bird that was getting dizzy and opened its eyes. "Oh, my brother birds fly away, fly, Ma'nabush is killing us one by one!" This bird was a duck and its wings made such a wrestling wind that those who could not hear his quacking opened their eyes.

Ma'nabush was angry. "Duck, for your not allowing me to do my killing you shall have red eyes and all your family from now on shall have red eyes." After all of this singing and the birds flying off, Ma'nabush was hungry. He buried the birds in a sandy spot by the river with their legs sticking up out of the sand. Over these he built his fire and he rested himself near the fire, putting his bottom closest to the fire. Ma'nabush fell asleep.

Two Winnebago had been out hunting and they came to the place where Ma'nabush was sleeping. They saw the smoke and moved close under cover of the bushes to see what caused the fire. They saw someone asleep near the fire and as they crept closer they saw that it was Ma'nabush.

One of the Winnebago hunters whispered to the other, "Let us steal the birds that Ma'nabush is planning to eat." The other agreed. They slowly crept low to pull the birds out from under the fire. They ate the birds and when they were ready to leave, they placed the birds' bones back under the sand with their legs sticking up into the air. Quietly they swept the ground around them with tree branches to avoid being followed.

After a long sleep, Ma'nabush woke up thinking that the birds must be cooked. When he pulled on the legs all he saw were the bones of the birds for all the meat was gone. Ma'nabush scratched his head as he dug deeper into the sand to find the meat of the birds. There was nothing there! Ma'nabush slapped his bottom. "You were supposed to keep watch! Someone stole our dinner while you were here to keep the fire and guard the food, bad bottom!"

Ma'nabush set out once again to find some food. He was very hungry and the day was disappearing into night. He came to a place where they was fruit hanging down over the bank of the river. He stooped over and saw that these were sweet cherries that were ripe and ready to be eaten. He dived into the water, but it was shallow and he struck the bottom, hurting his head badly.

Disappointed and bruised, he rested on the bank of the river. There he looked toward the sky and saw among the branches of the trees the wild cherries. He crawled up the tree and pulled on the branches to get the cherries that he wanted.

Ma'nabush continued on his journey, looking up he saw a Pa'skose or a buzzard. Pa'skose said to Ma'nabush, "How small you are down there."

Ma'nabush thought, "If I could only fly I could find food and a safe place to sleep." Ma'nabush stood in the clearing and flapped his arms in the air.

Pa'skose saw him and circled around to land on a tree top near by. "Ma'nabush, what are you doing? You cannot fly by flapping your arms you need wings to fly!" Ma'nabush shook his head at the buzzard. "I cannot fly and I really want to fly."

Pa'skose smiled. "What would you do if you could fly?"

"I would move much faster than I do down here on the ground. Take me up on your back, Brother Pa'skose, and let me see how everything looks from up there?"

Pa'skose let Ma'nabush climb onto his back. He lifted him up to the top of a very high mountain peak with steep sides and landed on a flat plateau. Pa'skose said to Ma'nabush, "We must rest here for my back is tired of carrying you. Look about and you can see the world." Ma'nabush stepped off of the buzzard's back only to have Pa'skose quickly fly away. Ma'nabush stared out at the earth around him, realizing that Pa'skose was not going to come back for him. Ma'nabush looked for a way to get down from the peak, but there was none, so he leapt down taking a jump forward to clear the rocks, he fell like an arrow to the earth.

He did not land on the earth though but he landed in a hollow tree. His people were camped not far away, but they didn't hear his cries for help. Ma'nabush was stuck in the tree for four days. The women from the camp decided that it was time to find more firewood and were walking looking for dried timber. They came to the hollow tree of Ma'nabush and were thinking of cutting it down when Ma'nabush decided it would be best if he made a sound of a porcupine. He called out, "a-he', ya-he', ya-he', ya-he." The women, hearing this, started with their axes cutting down the tree. Ma'nabush was frightened with the tree fell for he was sure they would continue to chop him into pieces. He decided to call out to the women. "Cut a small opening in the trunk and pull me out, I will show you my beautifully colored quills." The women did this only to pull out Ma'nabush! He ran away laughing at the women.

"The rest of this story of Ma'nabush will have to be told later," the teller said.

"It may be interesting for you to know that my great grandfather was a Menomini healer. He was invited to Washington, DC in eighteen ninety. This visit was to be a secret, but no one in Indian Country can keep a secret for long. He asked with four others for the people of Washington DC to come to our reservation at Keshena, Wisconsin to learn of our ways and beliefs. The first visit was followed by four more visits and there they learned about our social organization and government, customs, and systems of clans. Not everyone always told the truth for we didn't want them to know more than we did about ourselves. The people of that time lived on a reservation in the northeastern part of Wisconsin which was near where they first found their homeland near Nicollet in sixteen thrity-four, at least that is what the old ones say.

Once the Menomini lived beside the Winnebago, not the vehicle but the people, for our language was very similar to the Winnebago."

Sun Brother / Ojibwa

Finding this teller was not a simple task. The drive took three hours and night had fallen by the time the tree landmark was found. The smoke on the horizon was all there was to use as a directional and finally the dirt driveway came into view. The dark, purple sky held no moon and the only light came from the large front window which was covered by calico curtains. Carefully stepping around happy pups, I found the front door, but no knocker or door bell.

After rapping hard on the wooden door with my knuckles, footsteps were heard moving toward the front door. Slowly the doors opened but not easily for the hinges were rusted. The door could only open inches then it hit the linoleum floor and was stuck. A small child peered out from under long thick brown bangs. "Yeah, whachay-want?"

After a brief explanation, the father of the family came around from the back of the house to meet me. "Hi, sorry for the trouble." He extended his hand which was covered with cooking flour. "We're making pizza." He wiped his hands off on his black jeans which left distinguishable prints on his back side. "You said that you were raised on the rez, that meant you might come tonight or some other night, I wasn't sure. You're here now, so come on in. Dogs met you, huh? Oh, and the front door, ain't nobody used that in years. It's broke."

Inside the kitchen there were twelve people of all ages. Grandmother was at the wood stove making nasty remarks to the oven. Grandpa was sound asleep in a broken down easy chair in the comer, with a cat on his lap. The noise didn't affect him at all. Children of all ages were gathered around the kitchen table cutting up sausages, celery, mushrooms from a can, tomatoes, and slicing up an odd shaped meat substance.

Grandmother turned when she heard a stranger coming into her kitchen. "Hello, don't know why you came for our pizza, but it's better to come here than to call for carryout, although we don't have a phone! Hah, hah, hah, hah!" This was a happy group until a crying baby was heard from the depths of the house.

Leaning on the counter, I observed the pizza making. It was orchestrated with the best of performances. The long cookie sheet was filled with dough. It was passed around the kitchen table where everyone put whatever they wanted on a particular area. Then it went to Grandma, who had a hot pot of tomato sauce boiling on the hot wood stove. The smell of burning pine filled the air and mingled with the delicious smell of the pizza. The children ran into the other rooms of the house to play while the pizza cooked. Grandmother nodded to me as she carried a large basket of laundry into the room behind the hanging rug doorway.

The teller nodded to the chair across the table from him. "Sit down and take a load off." He rubbed his hands together, dropping dough on the table. "Good stuff pizza, even if it is homemade on the rez." He reached over to retrieve his soda. "I asked you to come out here 'cause I have to care for the kids mostly by myself. As you know, I work Tuesday through Saturdays in town, but it's not good telling stories in town. It's best to tell in a place where you feel safe."

He guzzled down soda as he bent toward the oven. Cautiously he pulled out his shirt tail to open the oven door. The room filled with a wonderful aroma. "My people are from the Northeast. I couldn't take it there. Everyone wants to be full blooded and milk the government for money. The winters there are brutal, but the real reason I came here is that the woman I fell in love with lived here in New Mexico. Couldn't find a way to make everything work, so here I am."

Flecks of cooking flour speckled his cheeks. "My wife died when the youngest was born, there wasn't time to get her to the hospital. My family is here now and here is where I'll stay." He smiled as he nodded to the back rooms of the house. "I tell my children about my people. How the Ojibwa are referred to as those who make pictures or pictographs and how they were also known as those who "puckered up" by neighboring groups of Indians. We once lived in the Northeastern part of the United States and Canada then moved from Maine to Montana, moving in and out of Missouri and the Dakotas."

His eyes moved to a photograph hanging on the wall by the empty telephone jack. "That's her. She was the most beautiful woman in the world. She was always happy, always filled with song, always there when you needed her." Leaning back in the chair, he shifted his gaze to the oven. "There is nothing more important in life than family."

He turned quickly to face me. "This is the story of my people, a proud people. You can check up on me if you want, although I'm sure this is the story you want to hear. I better hurry up or the pizza will bum!"

[The following story is consistent with the Bureau of American Ethnology and in Garrick Mallery's book, *Picture-Writing of the American Indians*, pgs. 255-256.]

The Story
of
Sun Brother

This is called Kwi-wi-sens wed-di-shi-tshi ge-wi-nip. In English it would be "little boy, his work." Ojibwa believe that life cannot function without the laws of nature. Nature brings up Sun. Sun will rise in the morning and set at night for as long as the spirits will it. Ojibwa believe Moon will rise and set whether it is seen or not, over and over again, as it is willed by the spirits.

Tcakabic was a trickster spirit and once he set a snare to catch Sun. He caught it and darkness came to the land, but not for long, for the wise spirits knew about Tcakabic's deed and sent a tiny, furry, brown mouse to bite through the snare. Mouse was courageous as he snuck up and bit right through the webbing with one bite. Sun raced back up into the sky, pleased to be free to rise and set. Sun was told to do this by the spirits, because in the beginning, Sun was put through many testings.

In the beginning, Ki'tshi Man'ido-Dzhe Man'ido, made the Mide Man'idos. There were only two men and two women, but they didn't know how to think. Dzhe Man'ido was saddened by this as he watched them make dumb choices and hurt themselves. Dzhe Man'ido decided to make them reasoning beings. This was good.

Dzhe Man'ido believed that these four were ready to lead more people. He lifted each one up and placed them in the palm of his large hand. Each stood cautiously for this was great magic. He told them to walk single file in a circle around his large palm. As they marched in their circle, more people mysteriously appeared behind them. The Later People became known as the Ojibwa. When the Later People, or Ojibwa were completely formed, Dzhe Man'ido's hand moved down to the earth to let them march off, but they ran and hid. Dzhe Man'ido was disappointed.

The Ojibway fought with the Mide Man'idos and many of the people on both sides became wounded, some died, 'and others were sick with fear.' There were those who were just miserable and they withered away to nothing. There are people like that today. Dzhe Man'ido became worried that all of the wisdom he had given to the Mide Man'idos would be lost if he didn't do something quickly. Dzhe Man'ido was the strong creator spirit, but there were wiser Spirits who had knowledge of the people. He called them for a conference, but none of them could find a solution to the people's behavior. It was agreed to share this problem with the Four Wind Spirits and they were called to the council. After a long discussion, it was decided to teach the people the wisdom of sacred medicine for sacred medicine would keep them alive. Sacred medicine would allow them to feel that they had some power over their own lives. But who would teach the people? The people had shown great fear at the sight of Dzhe Man'ido and he didn't want to scare them.

Dzhe Man'ido went to the Sun spirit who had magic to change the shape of his sunlight into that of a person. Sun Spirit agreed to help and sent down a ray of light in the form of a little boy. The little boy was directed to the house of a mother who already had one son. The woman accepted Sun Boy as an orphan and adopted him as her own. Sun Boy had piercing black eyes that shone night and day. When the fighting people looked into his eyes, they became peaceful. Slowly, the people put aside their weapons and began to work together. Sun Boy stayed with his adopted family and tried to fit in as a human boy would.

Every fall, the family went up into the mountains to hunt. During one hunt, the snows came early and Mother's own son became sick and died. The family decided to leave the hunting party and return home to bury their son. Each night, they set the dead son up on a blanket, held by tent poles, to prevent the wild animals from devouring his body. While the dead son was up on the blanket, Sun Boy played on the ground below with his bow and arrows.

The family was filled with grief and took no notice of Sun Boy.

Each night he heard the family cry as they mournfully sat to sing prayers to their dead son. Sun Boy was sorry for their sadness. The next night, Sun Boy stepped into the circle and told the family that he had the powers to bring the dead son back to life. Mother clicked her tongue at him, Auntie hid her eyes in shame, but Grandfather put out his hands, saying, "Come here, my son, how you would do this?"

Sun Boy explained, "Someone from this family should hurry back to the village to ask a woman there to make a wigwam out of birch bark. It needs to be ready when we arrive." Oldest cousin was chosen to return to the village at first light. Grandfather studied Sun Boy. "Then what do we do once we arrive at the bark wigwam?"

Sun Boy spoke carefully, "Dead brother should be placed in the middle of the birch bark wigwam in the ground." Mother began to cry. "Then, we would be accepting his death!"

Grandfather hushed her. "We must learn the ways of others. This one came to us for a reason. We must listen and learn from him."

Mother shook her head. "He's just a boy! What does he know of life and death?" Grandfather patted her hand. "Yes, what does he know of life and death? We shall see."

The next morning, when everyone was awake, oldest cousin left, running for the village. The family carried the dead boy. By late afternoon of the next day, they arrived to find in the middle of the village a birch bark wigwam. Oldest cousin met them. Proudly showing his family inside where the ground had been dug up to resemble a trough.

Sun Boy asked the family and all of the dead son's friends to enter the wigwam. They sat in a circle around the dead son. Sun Boy sat with them and waited. Everyone knew this was great magic and said nothing. They sat quietly for some time and then a shadow fell across them from the doorway. It was Bear! He pushed his way through the people to the feet of the dead son. As Bear rose up on his hind legs, the people quietly moved away from him.

Once Bear was standing up right, he began to wave his front paws in the air. The growling from his throat had a deep haunting noise that sounded like this, "HUUU, HUUU, HUUU, HUUU." Bear then leaned to the left, moving in a full circle around the dead boy. Each time Bear stopped, he would bellow, "HUUU, HUUU, HUUU, HUUU."

The first two times Bear did this nothing happened but the third time Bear moved around the body, it began to twitch. The fourth time Bear moved in his circle, the body of the dead son sat upright. As Bear continued to move toward the boy's feet, the son stood up alive!

Then Bear went down on all four paws and walked over to Grandfather. Bear spoke clearly to him, "My father is a spirit. You have a spirit son. We are both now of the spirit world. If you respect spirit power, smoke your tobacco and give thanks to all the spirits as you are now one yourself. This is the only time one shall be brought back to life. Be respectful of the spirits, learn of the ways of sacred healing and your people shall do well. This Now-Living-Boy has much to teach you. Listen, learn, and teach the ways of the sacred. It is with respect I leave my brother spirit to go home." Bear disappeared out the doorway and was gone!

Now-Living-Boy became Little Bear Boy. He was known to hold the wisdom of the spirits and knowledge of the Grand Medicine. Sun Boy and Little Bear Boy taught the knowledge of Dzhe Man'ido to the people. Little Bear Boy stayed with the people a long time, showing them, teaching them, healing them, and guiding them.

Sun Boy stayed only long enough to teach Grandfather his knowledge. Sun Boy met with his family one evening and told them, "It is time for me to go back to my home. Grandfather will hold the knowledge of healing. There will be no more magic to bring back the dead for I was only allowed to do this once. Always show respect and always pass your wisdom to those deserving. When you feel the warmth of Sun on you, know that I am watching over each one of you." Sun Boy walked outside and disappeared into a ray of light!

This is how we became wise once, now we need to become wise again.

The teller father went on to tell me about his views of Ojibwa medicine men. "My great uncle was a medicine man of the people and his name was known as Mah ca da o gun'h or The Black Nail. One time he went down the

Long Falls in his canoe, no one had done that before for it was too dangerous. He was always called for when someone was sick and their local medicine didn't work. Many would talk to him before they went out to hunt bear, because he knew how the bears think. People always paid him with something before he took care of them. His house was filled with goose down pillows, broken toasters, and sometimes people brought him pigs and chickens which he kept in a coop behind his house.

"He would do his curing of people's illness in the dark, in a wigiwam tightly covered with old mats to keep it dark and closed to outsiders. He first prepared himself by taking off all of his clothes in the dark wigiwam and then when he would come outside, he would be singing. The others around the wigiwam would start beating their drums and singing with him. No one could see him because it was dark. The wigiwam had bells, does' hooves, and antlers hanging from the inside of the roof. As my great uncle went inside the wigiwam it would begin to shake and rattle. Voices would be heard among the rattles and bells.

"One time my great uncle told me that he heard a deep rolling voice which was believed to be the Great Spirit and another time he heard this little squeaky voice which everyone knew was the Small Spirit. The Small Spirit is the interpreter for the Great Spirit and they usually travel everywhere together just for this reason. The sick person is inside the tent drinking his special tea and listening to the voices moving around him. Many say it was quite an experience to be healed by my great uncle.

"He called to the spirits when he entered the wigiwam by facing east first and addresses the ma'nidos who were supposed to know the best direction for healing. Then he would face south and call the ma'nidos from the south and then he turned to the west and finally the north. All of the ma'nidos have been called and arrive to help with his healing powers. The rattles used in the ceremony were known to start making noise all by themselves or with the help of the ma'nidos.

"Ma'nabush was the Menomini hero and he was also the grandson of Noko'mis one of the first spirits who founded the Mita'wit or Medicine

Society. His place was between the Great Unknown and the People of this Place. Ma'nabush comes from a combination of words - Masha means 'great' and wahbus which is the word for 'rabbit', a great rabbit that can do great deeds beyond what man can do. Noko'mis in everyday language means Grandmother of all men, but in the stories Noko'mis refers to the mankind of Ma'nabush and his brother Na'q'pote which means 'the earth.'

"Noqko'ma'ah is the other word for grandmother and all grandmothers were mothers of the earth and held the health of Ma'nabush between the Good Mystery and the Mita'wit or Grand Medicine. We have medicine and good health on our minds most of the time because if you lost your teeth or hurt your legs your chances of survival were pretty slim. We used to say,'Ah ni'bit t'sta ni'bua' which means 'if you lose your tooth you are dead!' Hah!

"It is much better to say, 'Nimi'tishim nina'bema'tes-i-m' which is' I am eating and I am alive!' The pizza is ready and you must stay to have some."

Earth Maker / Winnebago

Jim Pine Grayhair met me at the concession stand outside of the Albuquerque Pow-wow. He had on his head band of bright colors which complimented his bright yellow loin cloth and painted chest of wild colors. Jim didn't want a lot of attention placed on him as he had relatives nearby who probably wouldn't approve of his telling old stories.

[This story is consistent with the Bureau of American Ethnology, 37th Annual Report by Paul Radin.]

The Story of Earth Maker

Way before the beginning, Earth Maker was sitting in space when he became aware that there was nothing. He began to think of what he should do to change this and couldn't think of anything. This made him sad. He began to cry with tears flowing from his eyes. After a while he looked down and saw some bright objects that were his tears which had flowed below and formed the present waters.

Earth Maker began to think, "If I wish for something, it will happen just as my tears have become the oceans and seas." Then he thought again, "I wish for light, a big ball of light should float through the sky. Sometimes it will be high and other times this ball of light should sleep." The sun came to move across the sky only to disappear to the other side. "Oh, now we need a sister of the Sun to shine during the night. This ball of light must be not too bright or too dark." A soft light appeared in the night sky, but after several nights it would grow small and dim to disappear. "This is how women shall be, one minute they are soft and kind and then they become fierce and strong."

Earth Maker looked on the earth and he liked it except for the loud waves of the sea. He made the trees, but they did not make the waves quiet. On the four corners of the earth, he placed the four winds as great and powerful island weights for the earth was floating in his tears.   Still the earth was not quiet. He decided to make four long beings and threw them down to the earth where they pierced through the earth with their heads eastward. They were Snakes. The earth became very still and quiet. Then he looked upon the earth and saw that it was good.

Earth Maker sent four human like people from the above place to earth. When they arrived, they were all given one name as this made it easier to remember them. He Who Comes From Above, Walking in Mist, Comes in Mist, and a woman they called Drizzling Rain Woman. It is believed they came like spirits and there was a drizzling fog when the four came from above. Once here, one woman landed on some brushes. She was given the name She Who Bends the Brushes Down.

On the limb of an oak tree stood the birds of thunder called Thunderbird, White Thunderbird, and Black Thunderbird. Since they make the noise of the Tci wi they were known as Those Who Makes the Noise of the Tci wi. All of these became clans who were responsible for all things here.

Earth Maker took a piece of earth and made a specific shape. He stared at it and saw that it had no thoughts. "I hope there are NOT any more of you around," he said as he made it thoughtful. He spoke again, but it did not answer. "This is not good, you should show respect to your elders." He made a tongue and mouth. "Be careful how you use your mouth for you can get into serious trouble if are not careful!" Earth Maker tried to get it to speak, but it did not answer. "Oh, no, you have no spirit! I shall give you spirit, but use it wisely for your spirit is sacred and not to be abused." Earth Maker breathed into the being's mouth. The being spoke, "Thank you, for life."

Earth Maker felt proud enough to make three more beings. He made them powerful so that they might watch over the earth. These first four he made chiefs of the Thunderbirds. They were brothers, Kunuga, Henanga, Hagaga, and N'anyiga. He told them, "Look down on the earth for that is where you are going to live." He opened the clouds and placed them gently on the hard ground. "I give you this tobacco. It is for you to make me an offering out of respect for your lives. I shall gladly accept your prayers mixed with tobacco smoke and give you what you ask. This plant you most hold sacred for you must offer it to the Spirits out of respect."

Earth Maker gave them a wrapped bundle of fire. "I send this with you to use in life. When you send me an offering, this shall be your mediator. It shall take care of you throughout your life. It shall stand in the center of your dwellings and will be your grandfather. Respect fire or it will be your enemy."

The thunder spirits brought the four brothers down to earth. The oldest one, Kunuga said on his way down, "Brother, when we get to the earth and the first child is born a boy, we shall call him Chief of the Thunders." As night fell, second brother said, "When we get to the earth and a girl child is born, she shall be called Dark." They landed on an oak tree south of Red Banks near Green Bay called Within Lake. Standing On The Branches, the third brother said, "The first daughter born to me shall be called She Who Weighs The Tree Down Woman." Earth Maker shook his head for the first brothers were not as smart as he had wanted them to be.

The brothers jumped onto the earth, but the Thunder spirits did not touch the earth. The fourth and last brother said, "Brothers, the first son that is born to me shall be called He Who Alights On The Earth." The first thing they did on earth was to start their fire. Earth Maker noticed that he had not prepared food for these brothers. Carefully, Earth Maker thought of animals the people would be able to hunt. The oldest brother said, "What are we going to eat?" The younger brother took the bow and arrows that Earth Maker had given him and started walking eastward. The other brothers watched him, not knowing what he was going to do.

Later, the brother returned with a young deer on his back. He handed the bow and arrows to the next brother who later returned with a young deer, also. They were relieved that they had food. Remembering to show gratitude to Earth Maker, they cut off the ends of the deer tongues and the deer heart and threw them into the fire with some fat.

Their first visit was to the War Clan people who came from the west. Next they visited the Deer Clan, the Snake Clan, the Elk Clan, the Bear Clan, the Fish Clan, the Water Spirit Clan, and all the other clans that existed. As the clans sat around sharing stories, there appeared on the lake a white swan. When the other birds noticed the clan people were not going to hunt it, all the other birds came to visit. The clan people named them in the order of their coming until the lake was full.

Then the people began to dress the deer meat. Suddenly something came and landed on the deer meat. "What is that?" they said.

Kunuga, the eldest brother said, "It is a wasp, and the first dog that I will possess if it is black, I shall call Wasp. As the wasp smelled the deer dressing now the dog will smell the wasp." After the feast, the clans threw tobacco into the fire as an offering to Earth Maker. The brothers gave each clan some fire. At that place the people made their home. It was just the time of year when the grass comes as high as the knee.

One day, the brothers noticed something strange was near the camp, but they said, "We will leave it alone." In a little while, it moved nearer until it was in the camp and began to eat the deer bones. This became the dog named Wasp.

In the time of the beginning, the Thunder clansmen were as powerful as the Thunder spirits themselves. It was the Thunder people who made the ravines and the valleys for they wandered around the earth, striking the earth with their clubs to make dents in the hills. The upper clans were chiefs and the lower clans were the dog people.

One day the oldest of the brothers fell and did not get up again. He did not breathe and was cold. The three others asked, "What is the matter with our brother?" They waited for four days, but still he did not rise. The second brother was asked by his youngest brother what the trouble was, but he didn't know anything. He asked his third brother, but he didn't know. Then the two older brothers asked the youngest one, he didn't know. They began to mourn for him, not knowing what to do or think. They fasted and blackened their faces, as we do now when we are mourning. They made a platform and laid him on it. The snow fell and the three brothers filled their pipe and went to the east.

There they came to the First Being known as the Island Weight. Weeping, they came to him and said, "Grandfather, our brother Kunuga has fallen and is not able to rise again. Earth Maker made you great and endowed you with all knowledge and you know all things."

He answered, "My dear grandsons, I am sorry, I don't know anything about it. I refer you to the one ahead of me (the North). Perhaps he can tell you."

The weeping brothers went to North. He could not help them. "Perhaps the one in the West knows." They spoke to the West, but he could not help. He referred them to the South. When they reached the fourth and last one, they entered the lodge and there sat the three they had asked before. All Direction Spirit answered, "Grandsons, the Earth Maker has willed your brother to not rise. Whenever one reaches the age of death, they shall die. Your brother will be in a village in the West where your clan will go after this place. He will be in charge of all of you and when the world has ended your brother shall take all of you to Earth Maker. Now go home."

The Thunder brothers thanked the four Spirits and left the tent. When they got home, they took their brother's body, dressed him in his best clothes, and painted his face. They told him where he was to go and buried him with his head facing to the west with his war club. They placed a branch of a tree at his grave with a red painted stick so that nothing should cross his path on his journey to the spirit place. They filled his pipe with the sacred tobacco to take along with him on his journey. Also, the life he left behind and the victories he might have gained were given to his relatives.

"According to the Winnebago Creation myth when Earth Maker The Creator of Earth came to consciousness and began creating life, the earth (which we were to live on) was in continual motion. Then he decided to stop the spinning with his four enormous snakes, or four water spirits. These "Island Weights" seem to be identical with the four cardinal points and are not to be confused with the Four Winds mentioned later."

"The place of the Winnebago kept changing," Jim Pine Grayhair continued after he finished the story. "The French pushed the Winnebago all over the east coast in the 1800s. They were moved to what is now known as southern Wisconsin except they were on a tract west of Sugar River that was claimed by the Sauk and Fox tribes. This made the land very crowded and the delegates saw that this was not good. They put the Fox River between these tribes to have surveillance over them and to keep them from moving into New York Indians. A treaty was drawn up by a Mr. Trowbridge on August 18th in 1821 with the understanding that five hundred dollars was to be paid to the Menomonee and Winnebago and fifteen hundred dollars would be paid the following year to them for goods.

"Ten days later after the agreement was signed, the Menomonee and Winnebago came together to meet their new neighbors the Not'to-ways or the New York Indians and to receive their fifteen hundred dollar payment in goods as agreed upon. There were wild Indians, young and old Indians, women with papooses, everyone eager to have the good life. The payment of the fifteen hundred dollars worth of goods was made with a big ceremony and all the delegates introducing each other with speeches. All of this was followed by a feast, dancing, laughing and great fun for several days.

"It did not end well, though, for in 1831 the United States government put forth another treaty that set the boundaries claiming that all lands east of Fox River, Green Bay, and Lake Winnebago and from Fond du Lac south eastern to the Milwaukee River down to the mouth belonged to the United States. They claimed everything west of Green Bay to Plover Portage in Wisconsin. The officials wrote about how this country was ceded to the United States for the benefit of all Indians in this area. Now I am here and this is good, I like this Pow-wow and hope you watch me dance."

First Born / Papago

Long John Shorty slowly scanned the green Formica cafe tables searching for a woman with short brown hair and a pink carnation. When he spotted me, he frowned. He wiped his long brown fingers on his faded blue jeans, pulled down his white button work shirt, then pushed back his gray stained Stetson hat. His boots held deep creases from wear.

"Howdy, ma'am." His right hand extended to mine. "Hello, Long John Shorty?" My soft voice sounded weak next to his rolling deep voice.

"Pleasure, ma'am. Thought since you was drivin' all the ways out here, the least I could do is meet you. Since you're buy'n me lunch an all." He slid into the booth opposite mine at the table.

"It's good to talk to someone about what's goin' on round here. The government's done dammed up the water for Phoenix to get them swimming pools all filled up and left us down here with no water, none at all." He frowned, reached up and took his hat off to place it next to him on the table. He waited for me to say something, as if he had been too forward. "Yes," I nodded, "Please, let's order so you won't be late getting back to work. Tell me all about what's going on." I placed a menu in front of him.

"Well, we's always had water, that's our way. Grew our own, ate our own, sold what we had too much of, then them folks up in richville decided they needed our water. They dammed up the river, took our water, left our folks without land to work, everyone got hungry, plenty died, then the government sent people down here with food stamps. People started eaten' the wrong food, got fat, got diabetes, and then they died all over again." He brushed his long black bangs out off of his forehead. Looking at the menu, he smiled. "They got chicken fried steak. Do you think I could have some of that?"

"Sure," I said smiling. "You can have what every tickles your fancy."

Long John Shorty let out a deep guttural laugh. "Hot dog, you must be rich or something." I laughed with him.

After we ordered, Long John Shorty pulled out a pencil from his pocket. He tapped it on the table as he spoke, as if he was keeping time to the rhythm of his words. "This here is the story we was taught, many of us remember stuff from the old guys, the ones who talked all the time, telling us not to forget.

"Then they took the land away and what was the point of remembering?" He put his hat back on, as if he was naked without it. "Here then is the story, I ain't say'in it's right, I ain't say'in it's wrong, but this here is what I got."

The Story of First Born

Long ago, they say, when the earth was not yet finished, darkness lay upon the water and that darkness rubbed. The sound it made was like the sound on the edges of a pond. There on the water in the darkness, in the noise and in a very strong wind, a child was born. The child lay upon the water and did as a child does for the water rocked it softly to keep the child quiet. The wind always blew and carried the child everywhere. Whatever made the child took care of him, fed him, and raised him.

One day he got up and found something stuck to him. It was algae. So he took some of the algae and from it, he made termites. Then he sent termites out to get more of the algae to be put in one place so he could sit down on it and think about things to do. And the little termites did that for the First Born One. The termites gathered a lot of algae and First Born tried to decide how to make a seat that the wind would not blow anywhere. This is the song he sang: Earth Medicine Man finished the earth.

Come near and see it and do something to it.

He made it round.

Come near and see it and do something to it.

In this way, First Born finished the earth. Then he made all animal life and plant life. There was no sun or moon and it was always dark. The living things didn't like the darkness, so they got together and told First Born to make some light. Then the people would be able to see each other and would live contentedly with each other.

First Born said, "All right, you name what will come up in the sky to give you light."

They discussed it thoroughly and finally agreed that it would be named "Sun". But about then Coyote came running and said, "It rose! It rose! It will be named 'Light'. But nobody agreed. The sun rose and went over to one side, but it didn't light up the whole earth. Then it went down and it was dark. So the First Born one sang like this:

Didn't we make the sun and talk with it?

Hihih.

Didn't we made the sun and talk with it?

Hihih.

Then it began to get light again and First Born said, "The sun will rise and come overhead." It did as he said, but it came very low and hot. First Born sang again and pointed to another place, saying that the sun would come up there and not burn anyone or be too bright.

Next he made the moon and stars, and the paths that they always follow. Now the living things could see themselves. Some were large and some very small, some were very fast and some very slow. Many of them were dissatisfied with themselves. Those that were small wanted to be large and those that were slow wanted to be fast.

Along came Black Beetle, who said, "Soon the living things will multiply and crush me with their feet because I'm not a fast runner and have no way to save myself. I think that when someone has lived a long time he should die and go away and never come back here again. That way the earth will never get overpopulated and no one will crush me."

At that time Rattlesnake's bite was harmless. The children would catch rattlesnake and fling him about like a toy. When they were tired they would sit on him and rip out his teeth. He never slept for he was fearful of the children. He asked First Born, "The children are making my life miserable. You must make me different so I can live safely somewhere."

First Born changed many of the animals. He took Rattlesnake's teeth out and threw them away. They landed and grew into what we now call, "Rattlesnake's Teeth Plant." As the sun rose its rays beamed over the horizon. First Born grabbed two rays of sunlight and threw them into the river. When he took them out of the water they were teeth for the rattlesnake. "Now, I have done this for you. If anything comes near you, bite it and kill it. From now on the people will be afraid of you. You will not have any friends and will always crawl alone."

Then the sun rose in the place it is now, and First Born looked at it and sang:

First Born made the earth.
First Born made the earth.
Go along, go along, go along.
It's going along.
Now all will remain as it is.

When he finished his song, he told everyone and every animal where they would be living. Some would live in the forests, some in the mountains, and some would live in the valleys. He also said this, "I have finished all things and they will always be as they are now."

In the East, the singing and dancing had begun for those that will die here. They will go to the singing and dancing ground. The land around the dancing ground will be beautiful. There will be plenty of prickly pears and the people will always be happy.

That's the way First Born prepared the Earth for us. Then he went away.

Long John Shorty smiled when lunch came. The chicken fried steak was quickly eaten. He tipped his hat and went back to work.

Sacred Star Siblings / Osage

"This is a very complicated adventure you want me to take!" The seventy year old face wrinkled with his smile. The soft afternoon breeze blew his white bangs across his forehead. "I'm not sure I am up to this, to be honest. But if you want to hear this, you must not interrupt me or I will get lost."

He pulled a red bandanna from his back blue jean pocket. Lifting it to his mouth, he wiped his dry lips. Slowly, he let his hands rest in his lap and with a deep breath, he began his adventure.

The Story of Sacred Star Siblings

Beneath the River of Life, which is high in the sky, there was the male killing animal known as Morning Star which is a red star. In the sky, there were six stars called the Elm Rod in a group of four, then the Evening Star, and Little Star. Beneath these were moon, seven stars, and the sun. The seven stars were the peace pipe and the war hatchet constellations. The last one was close to the sun and the first one was near the moon which was on the same side. Four layers or upper worlds existed, ancestor people passed through them on the way to earth.

The lowest of the upper heavens rested on an oak tree and the ends of the other levels were supported by pillars or ladders. The tradition began below the lowest heaven, on the left side, under the peace pipe. Each space that the people climbed down corresponded to a sacred chant. Each chant had four parts. The first chant preceded the arrival of the first heaven, pointing to a time when the children of the 'former end' of the race were without human bodies as well as human souls. A bird hovered overhead, watching the travels of the people. That was when birds were given human souls in their bird bodies.

The people moved down to the fourth heaven, the one closest to the earth. Finally, the people moved down to the third. When the people stood on the earth it was a beautiful day. The earth was covered with rich vegetation. From the time of landing on earth, the Osage separated into groups. There were those who went to the right and became a warring people. There were others who went to the left and were peace keeping people. People had no bodies at this time and they did not eat. The people were fearful for they didn't know what would happen to them.

The peaceful people met the black bear, Kaxe-wahil-sa in the distance. He offered to become their messenger. They sent him to the different stars to ask for help and guidance. Kaxe-wahil-sa visited the stars in this order: Morning star, sun, moon, seven stars, evening star, and little star. Finally, Kaxe-wahil-sa visited Wacinka-aitse, a female red bird sitting on her nest. Wacinka-aitse was also known as grandmother. She listened to Kaxe-wahil-sa. Wacinka-aitse gave all the people human bodies, making them out of her own body.

The people built an earth lodge as a place of gathering for the warring people. Buffalo skulls were on the top of the lodge and the bones of the animals which they killed whitened on the ground. The very air was thick with decaying bodies and animals.

"Ah, but that is another long adventure!" my storyteller said. "This is all I know of the Beginning Time, but it is important to know the way of the Osage people, some were warriors and some were peace keepers."

NOTE: **Osage** - Oh-Sage call themselves the Pa-he'-tse meaning "those on the mountain."

"There were two groups, the Big Osage and the Little Osage, who were known as the Arkansas Band. There are part of the Siouan Language Family. The Osage once lived in the northwest comer of the Arkansas Indian Territory where they came into contact with the Comanche. They also lived near the western state boundary of Kansas where they were in contact with the Kiowa, Cheyenne, and Arapaho. They were moved to the Osage Indian Reservation in the late 1880s by the United States Government.

"There was a time when the Cherokee and the Seneca wanted to join forces with the Osage, but they soon learned that we are not that friendly. When the Seneca came to talk to the Osage, as the story goes in 1816 or around there, the Osages said that they had to think about it. The Shawnee decided to come and talk a peace agreement with the Osages just after that and the Osage said, 'Come tomorrow about the middle of the day and we can talk business.' Then the Osage said, 'The Great Spirit has been good to us and we are feeling generous.'

"The Seneca went to speak to the Shawnee because they were the first to attempt to try and speak with the Osage, but the Shawnee said they were the ones who were invited. The Shawnee went to the meeting with the Osage and while they were there an old man came up to them. He told them to leave for the Osage were thinking of killing them all. The Shawnee hurriedly left the area and as they were moving north they came to the Seneca. The Seneca told them about the Osage being tricksters and to ignore the old man and go back to the meeting.

"While the Seneca were moving back into the camp of the Osage they overheard some Osage talking about killing them. The Seneca took off running but they could hear the Osage behind them. The Seneca dropped their packs of food and goods they wanted to share with the Osage to just run as fast as they could. Soon they met up with the Shawnee. The two groups agreed to leave the Osage alone. The wise man of the Shawnee evidently gave a speech which to this day the Osage remember his words, he said, 'The Osage shall be like a lone cherry tree standing in the prairies where the birds of all kinds shall light on it at pleasure but the Osage shall be alone like an herb standing alone in the garden.'

"The Kiowa used to call us the A;'laho' but if they were angry at us they called the Osage K'apa'to and I am not going to translate either one of these for they are not complimentary names! We ended up with the Omaha, Ponka, and Kansa people. There were certain beliefs and practices that we had in common. For instance we did not worship our ancestors and we were very respectful to our elders and those of our group speaking to them in a formal manner, also we did speak of the dead often even days, weeks, years after they had died. There were no worries about the dead coming back to haunt us for we didn't have any totems or statue worship. Our mothers did scare us with stories of the people from the dead coming back just to see us if we were bad and there were times when they told us we behaved like a bad spirit. All of us used tobacco as a sacred smoke during prayers, but we didn't abuse it as something that would bring spirits to our way of thinking, at least I don't think we did.

"My grandmother used to tell us that if someone eats the large intestine of cattle known as tas'iyaka their face will break out in boils. Boils will be on some covered part of the body not on the hands or face. If a person decided to become intimate with another then these boils would be seen. She also told us that if a man eats a liver of a female dog or if a woman eats the liver of a male dog, the face of the person who ate the liver will break out in nasty sores and ooze pus. Grandmother's famous belief was if a person steals they will grow warts on their hands and if their palate begins to peal in their mouth, it is from telling lies. My grandfather told us as children that if we dreamt of goats we would walk as goats, run as goats and be able to climb straight up mountains just like a goat.

"Finally my aunt stated to all of us when we were leaving home to listen for the Whip-Poor-Will bird at night. If it sings and we tell it to stop and it does then someone in our family will die but if the bird continues to sing our family is safe. We have been on our own since the beginning with the stars. It is difficult for people to get close to the Osage, hah!"

Turtle, Earth-Namer and Father of the Secret Society / Maidu

"Tie your shoe." The little boy bent down to gather up his shoe laces. His father sat straight and stern in the cafe's window booth. "Telling these stories has something to do with us dying *out,* right?"

He was given a summary of my purpose in collecting stories and was surprised. "You mean you want to preserve these for the younger generation? What about their parents and grandparents? Shouldn't they be the ones telling these stories to their children?"

His dark eyes studied the activity in the cafe. It was high noon in downtown Albuquerque. People were milling around talking on cell phones while waiting to be seated. Waitresses raced back and forth from the kitchen carrying trays of food while the bus boys lugged around tubs of dirty dishes. There were peals of laughter mixed with undertones of business discussions all around us. Finally, the waitress arrived with our tray of food. Sustenance is a great instigator for conversation. The speaker quickly devoured everything on his plate. Quietly, he watched his son eat the last of his French fries.

"Well, I suppose it couldn't hurt to have other people know of our beginnings, but I would think they would be busy trying to remember their own." His strong hands pushed the ice tea glass to the center of the Formica green table. "My wife doesn't remember much about her family, but then she doesn't remember much of anything, does she son?" The little boy methodically nodded in agreement.

"I would like to think this story is sacred, meant only for my people, you understand. This isn't something to make money off of or to treat as a joke. This is our way, our belief, our choice of life, not something to banter about and wonder about in colleges."

Wiping his mouth with the paper napkin, he leaned back to watch the people at the other tables. "I don't want anyone to know I told you this story, not anyone! My wife says I'm too strict, but one can't be too careful nowadays. You appear to be honest and sincere or I wouldn't be talking to you."

The little boy leaned against his father, lifting his father's arm over his shoulders. "All right, I will tell this story, which is not a story, but a real truth, a firm way of knowing. Maybe it will help other people who feel they know the right way and everyone else is a fool."

Stretching his legs out in the aisle, he pushed back his cowboy hat and started. His story was confirmed with Colin Taylor's book, *Native American Myths and Legends*.

The Story of Turtle, Earth-Namer and Father of the Secret Society

*A*t first there was no light. There was reason for no light. There was no sun, no moon, no stars, nothing to give light. Everything, everywhere, all the time then, was water. Water is the womb of life. Somewhere, no one knows from where, came a raft floating on the water. It came from what is now known as the north. There were two people who sat on the raft. They were Turtle from the North and Father of the Secret Society. The raft floated. Turtle sat quietly on the raft for a long time. Soon he was tired and he told Father of the Secret Society, "This is enough. It is time for us to get off this raft. All this floating around is making me tired and we can't see anything, we don't know if we will be eaten or drown."

Father off the Secret Society said nothing. Father of the Secret Society is not supposed to say anything unless it is important. Turtle said nothing for a time, and then he had to speak, "Aren't you hungry? Wouldn't you like to get off this raft? Aren't you as tired as I am? How do we know where we are going?" Turtle from the North was upset and spoke for some time. Father of the Secret Society said nothing. After many years a rope fell from the sky. Down the rope came Earth Namer or Earth Initiator.

He slid down the rope and landed on the raft. This gave Turtle quite a scare. "Who are you? Where did you come from? Are you going to eat us? Did you bring food? Who are you?"

Earth Namer waited until Turtle from the North had finished

speaking. Earth Namer was polite. "I am Earth Namer and I am here to make the Earth."

Turtle felt around for there was a glow coming from Earth Namer's head. Turtle felt a basket over Earth Namer's head. "Why do you have a basket on your head? Are you dangerous?"

Earth Namer held the basket firmly on his head while Turtle from the North pushed it around. "Leave the basket alone! My head is so bright if I take this basket off it will blind you. Leave me alone!"

Turtle did so. They floated for a while then Turtle spoke, "Father of the Secret Society and I have been floating a long time. We are hungry, sick of all this water and we would like to get off this raft. Can you help us?"

Earth Namer sat down on the raft and waited for Turtle to finish. "Yes, I can help you. I have come from above, up in the sky. There will be people here, but first we must make land. Then you can get off the raft."

Turtle pondered on these things. Then he asked, "When are the people coming? Will they be nice people? When are you going to make the land?"

Earth Namer answered, "I don't know when the people are coming and I don't know what they will be like. First we have to find a way to get some mud or dirt and then we can make land."

Father of the Secret Society said nothing. He sat and listened for he had nothing to say. Turtle from the North came up with a plan. He said to Earth Namer, "Why don't you tie the rope around my middle, here, and I will dive down into the water and find what it is flowing over. If there is some mud I will find it." Earth Namer agreed although he knew the water was very deep, it would be nice to have some quiet for a time. Earth Namer tied the rope around Turtle from the North.

Turtle pulled on the knot. "When I tug on the rope once it means the rope is too short and will be of no use. If I tug on the rope twice, like this, pull me up for I may be so tired I can't swim anymore, but I will have some earth." Earth Namer nodded.

Turtle from the North dove into the water. He was gone six years. Finally Earth Namer felt a tug on the rope then another tug. He pulled the rope up rapidly. Turtle from the North was covered in green slime, for he had been down a long, long time. There was earth under his nails, for what he had carried had been washed a way.

Earth Namer took his knife out from under his left arm pit and cleaned Turtle from the North's fingernails. He put the earth in the palm of his hand and rolled it around until it was a small pebble of mud. Earth Namer laid it on the raft. They continued to float.

Every now and then they would look at the mud pebble. It was the same size, it did not grow. The third time they looked at it, the pebble was as big as the distance between his two hands when his arms were extended. The fourth time, it had grown to the size of the earth today. The raft came aground and all around there were shapes, but it was dark. The raft became still at the place called Ta'doiko'.

Turtle from the North stood on the still raft. "Why can't we see?! It is still dark! I am tired of this now. We have worked hard to have land and now we can't see a thing because it is too dark. Do something!"

Earth Namer studied his two companions. Father of the Secret Society still said nothing, nothing at all. What had happened was magical, but Father of the Secret Society had nothing to say. Turtle from the North was never short of words and something had to be done to keep him quiet. Earth Namer said to Turtle from the North, "Let's get off this raft and see what we can find."

Earth Namer stood on the land and said, "I will ask my sister to come up." A light shone very dimly in the east. Then all of a sudden Father of the Secret Society stood off the raft and started screaming. He was screaming at the top of his lungs! The sun came up and went down. After the sun went down, Father of the Secret Society began to cry. Again it was very dark. Earth Namer was surprised at Father of the Secret Society, but then he had been traveling with Turtle from the North much longer than anyone. Earth Namer called to his brother, asking him to come up. Then the moon rose.

Earth Namer asked Turtle from the North and Father of the Secret-Society, "How do you like my brother?" Surprisingly they both answered, "He is very good."

Then Turtle from the North spoke up again, "Is that it? Is that all your going to do? Is that all the light we get?"

Earth Namer shook his head. "No, I will do more." He called to the stars, each by name, and they came to light in the sky.

When this was done Turtle from the North asked, "Now, what do we do?"

Earth Namer answered him, "Wait and I'll show you."

Earth Namer made a tree grow at Ta'doiko. There Turtle from the North, Earth Namer, and Father of the Secret Society sat in the shade of the tree for two days. After this, they set off to see the earth and what it was doing. They started off at sunrise and were back by sunset. Earth Namer traveled so fast that all they could see was a ball of fire flashing about under the ground and in the water.

One day as they were out exploring, Coyote and his Rattlesnake dog came up out of the ground. When the three returned they found Coyote and Rattlesnake dog under their tree. The five built huts to live in, here at Ta'doiko. They would visit each other, but none of them could go inside Earth Namer's hut.

In the morning, Earth Namer made all the trees and plants. He took some mud and made the first deer, which turned out all right, so he made more animals. There were times some of the animals were very strange looking. Turtle from the North would say, "Earth Namer, this animal will never be able to walk or eat. You need to change him. This won't do the way he is now!" Earth Namer would listen and correct his mistakes thanks to Turtle from the North.

Turtle from the North became busy teaching animals, water creatures, birds, bugs, and burrowing animals how to live.

On an afternoon walk with Coyote, Earth Namer decided he would make people. "They will be made out of mud." This is what Earth Namer decided. He returned to Ta'doiko, took dark red earth, mixed it with water and made two figures. One was a man and the other was a woman. He laid the man on his right and the woman on his left inside his house. Earth Namer lay back between the two of them with his arms stretched out over his head. He did this all afternoon and night which caused him to sweat and shake at times.

Early in the morning the woman began to tickle him. Earth Namer kept very still, it was difficult but he didn't laugh. Finally he couldn't stay still anymore. He got up and walked about. Then he took a piece of wood and thrust it into the ground, starting a fire. There before him were two shockingly white people. They had white skin, white lips, white teeth, pink eyes, black hair, and a light about them. No one to this day has seen anyone this white!

The man was called Ku'ksu and the woman, Morning Star Woman. They walked out of Earth Namer's hut to look around. Coyote saw them and laughed. "They don' have hands! You will have to give them hands like mine!"

Earth Namer shook his head. "No, I will give them hands like their creators, mine." Coyote asked, "Why?" Earth Namer said, "If they get chased by bears they can climb a tree! That is why, leave me be!"

Coyote pestered Earth Namer wanting to know how he had made these people. Earth Namer became irritated with Coyote and finally told him. Coyote laughed. "Oh, is that all? I can make people, too!" Coyote made the people in his hut. He lay down with his arms out over his head and waited. He fell asleep, and then was awakened by the woman tickling his ribs. He tried not to move, but he couldn't help himself, he started laughing and laughing and had to move.

In the morning there were two glass eyed people staring at him. Earth Namer was very disappointed. "I told you not to move! You moved and this is why they have glass eyes!"

Coyote told the first lie, "I didn't move, they just are that way." Earth Namer had no reason to speak to Coyote again. Father of the Secret Society taught the people how to chant and to show respect to the Creator, but he did this with his magic and not his voice.

Earth Namer told Ku'ksu to take all the newly made people to the lake. When Ku'ksu got there he would be Old Man. Ku'ksu did as he was told and by the time he reached it, he was Old Man. He fell into the lake and sank, out of sight. Soon after this the ground began to shake, like an earthquake. There was a roaring which came from under the water and Ku'ksu came standing out of the water as a young man.

Earth Namer told the people," If you do as you are told, life here will be good. When any of you grow old all you have to do is come to this lake, or get someone to bring you to the lake and go down into the water and you will become young. But, you must follow the rules I give you or there will be trouble."

Famous last words, yes? Earth Namer then went away. He left in the night and went up to the place from which he had originally come.

All this time food was easy to acquire. Women set out their food baskets before bed and in the morning they were filled with food. Life was good.

Coyote came along and he asked the People how they were doing. They told him, "Life is good. We sleep, find our food ready for us, walk around, eat and go back to sleep." Coyote frowned. "This is not the way to live! Let me show you something better."

Coyote explained to the people how to have a foot race. The people were excited to do something different and they gambled and raced all night. Rattlesnake Dog went into Ku'ksa's hut and asked him, "What do we do now? Coyote will ruin everything!"

Ku'ksu said nothing. Rattlesnake Dog went out and along the course the racers were running, he hid in a hole. Just his head stuck up out of the hole. Coyote's only child began to run in the foot race and was in the lead, when he raced over Rattlesnake Dog's head, his foot hit Rattlesnake Dog's mouth. Coyote's son fell dead.

Coyote was cheering and clapping at the home stake. He just knew his son would win. Another runner raced up to him and said, "Coyote, your son is fallen and I believe he is dead. He does not move nor do his eyes show any light."

Coyote laughed at the runner. "No! My son cannot die, you only tell me this to trick me!" The people brought Coyote's child down the mountain to him. He was dead. Coyote cried and cried. This was the first death. People didn't understand why Coyote's eyes leaked and why he was sad. Coyote took his child and placed him in the lake. But there was no noise, nothing happened, the body drifted around on the surface for four days and then began to sink.

On the fifth day Coyote took four sacks of beads and gave them to Ku'ksu, pleading with him to bring his child to life. Coyote cried, begged, and brought more gifts for five days.

This fifth day, Ku'ksu took all the gifts Coyote had brought him and placed them on the ground outside of his hut. He told them to bring the body. He put the body on a bear-skin and wrapped it carefully. Ku'ksu got on his knees and dug up the earth until there was a deep hole. He put the body into it and carefully covered it with dirt, packing it firmly down. Ku'ksu spoke, "This is the way you must place the dead until the world is made again."

A year later the earth changed. Everyone spoke the same language. The night before spring, the people had a burning to give thanks and to show respect for the dead. In the middle of the burning their languages changed. Some couldn't understand the others, and others could understand some, but not their neighbors. This was confusing. Each man and his wife and children spoke the same language, though.

In the morning, Ku'ksu brought the people together. Since he spoke all the languages he could communicate with all of them. "Now you will learn the names of the different animals, plants, birds, as well as learn to hunt and care for yourselves. When this is finished you will be sent to different places to live. You will no longer live together, but separate from now on.

"The warriors are to go to the north, the singers to the west, the flute players to the east, and the dancers to the south. Go, find your way and live well."

The people did as they were told. Ku'ksu and his wife were left alone, until she decided to go and live with those at Marysville Buttes. Ku'ksu went to the spirit house and sat down on the south side. There he found Coyote's child sitting on the north side. The door was on the west side of the spirit house. From there our stories tell of our customs and the ways of death. This is all there is to know about creation. It is sad the Turtle-from-the-North no longer speaks our language for I am sure we could learn much from him. Coyote had followed Ku'ksu to the spirit hut and when he entered he saw his son. Coyote ran out of the spirit hut through the people, calling out to them, "Ku'ksu has shown me how to be with my son! I must kill myself and then all will be well."

Coyote ran to a high mountain and threw himself off of a high cliff. He crashed below, making a terrible noise on the way down. Then he ran to the hut to be with his son, but Ku'ksu and his son were gone. Coyote was terribly sad and ran to the west. The people never saw him again. Ku'ksu and Coyote's son had gone up to the place of Earth-Namer. That is what happened and is believed what happens to good people today.

"The Maidu live in California, but we are not air heads like some people I could mention!" The storyteller said, "My family was known to be part of the Nisenan who live in the southern half of California. There are three language groups of the Maidu: Knokow, Maidu, and Nisenan. We love to trade clam disc beads, dry salmon, and eat pine nuts. My grandfather and grandmother lived in a semi-subterranean shelter which was safe for when the fires or the rains would come, they would close their door and be completely safe.

"I am glad to introduce you to my people and our ways for so few people know about us. We have great artists with an excellent tourist center, come on over and meet my people!"

The Ghosts of the Ponka and the Omaha

Frank LeFech related a story that had been documented by his family back in the 1880s. He felt it important the old words be remembered aloud rather than just written in the old family Bible. Frank was very superstitious and worked hard to be a disbeliever, but as he spoke his eyes grew wide and frightened. His family trained him well in the ways of the old ones. This story was researched with Mooney's work and found to be mostly correct.

The Story of The Ghosts of the Ponka and the Omaha

Four nights after a death, the ghost of the dead person had to travel a very dark road. After they got to the end of the road they would reach the Milky Way which was filled with light. The people tried to help the dead by keeping the lighting fires burning along the road away from the grave sites for four days and nights. After going along the Milky Way, the ghost of the dead would come at last to a fork in the road.

There an old man sat, clothed in a buffalo robe with the hair on the outside of it. The old man would say nothing to the dead ghost but would point to the road the dead ghost should take. One road was a very short one and he who followed it would soon come to the place where the good ghosts lived. The other road was an endless one. Along other dead ghosts were crying and crying from exhaustion.

There was once a man who was hit with lightening. He had to be buried face down with the soles of his feet split wide open. When this was done the man could go to the spirit land of the ghosts and never gave any trouble to the land of the living. There are those who don't make it to be a ghost, but are taken away to live with the place of the animals. This was believed to go way back to becoming one with the ancestors who were animals in the beginning. These animal ghosts are hunted, killed, and skinned which is a terrible fate for anyone who believes they have lead a good life.

When a man is killed in battle, the thunder is supposed to pick up his ghost spirit and take it up into the sky. One time my father saw thunder on the ground walking with beaded moccasins. There have been sorcerers who work on the battle fields. There was a story of a sorcerer who prepared a love potion for each person who bought one. When they were good and polite to the one they loved, life was good but when they were disrespectful and ugly they would die. This was used to keep men who were not in love with a woman they were courting from continuing in the relationship.

It is important that if you make a very special meal for a very special occasion to put some of this food outside around the house before you go to bed for the ghosts of your family to feed. Some do not remember this and the ghosts will come into the house at night searching for a way to get some of the special food from that special occasion. There are some ghosts who want to be seen and others you can only hear or feel, but cannot see for they do not want to frighten you or to scare your memory of them.

The dead ghosts of people who wander far from where they were born float upward to go to the place of the caves in the mountains. There they move forward and never look back for to look back would make them permanently stuck here forlorn and lost, wandering and without hope. Those who continue on without looking back or thinking of those who have turned into ghosts before them shall do well and take the short road to the good ghost place. One should never wish the dead back with them for this surrounds them with death and despair. In life we move forward and in death it is vital to move forward on the path to goodness and not look back on what has happened in the past.

The sun can hold dead ghosts as well as the moon and all the stars. This would be a good place to be for the rest of time, but we are human and our lives are confused with the church, traditions, and our personal beliefs. I do believe that all my relatives are on the short road and their ghost spirits are good.

Coming of Creation / Koksoagmyut

"**H**ey, didn't think that you were going to show!" The two young women leaned against their men friends laughing as I shook off the winter snow from my boots. The December snow had kept me from going down my familiar streets to the Indian Pueblo Cultural Center downtown on Twelfth Street. "You Pueblo reservation women don't know nothing about snow do you?" I shook my head and frowned.

"We are from the north coast and we really get snow out there. This snow here is just a thought. We get a release of spiritual white stuff! You really want to hear an old story or were you just fooling around with us the other day?"

Pulling my wet jacket off, I answered him firmly, "Yes, I seriously want to hear an old story and since you are already in the mood to talk, why don't we sit upstairs and I can treat everyone to some hot chocolate?"

The four were delighted to be given a nice warm treat on this cold afternoon. The older man was anxious to tell this story and he appeared to have been a singer for he had a cadence to his voice when he spoke. "I teach the history of my people up by Koksoak or the South River which is several hundred miles long and takes loops around lakes and across the highlands down to Quebec. If you come to visit us be sure you come by steamer, it is easier to get in and out through the bay."

The younger man raised his finger at the table. "Yes, we are at longitude 68`16` west of Greenwich and 58`8` north, on the right bank of the Koksoak river about 27 miles from its mouth."

"Thank you, Albert. Now she can find us if she is in a pinch. Now back to the story. The early Moravian missionaries tried to convert the people in our area into being Christians. In 1825, a vessel came up the Koksoak River for the purpose of founding a new missionary station opposite Fort Chino for it could serve as a beacon with its high walls. The locals were endearing people and the whole event was a success. The Hudson Bay Company built a trading post on the river and a small party was sent from Moose Factory to start another trading post to develop housing for the new developments expected in 1831.

"The men remained there working and building up the community. The ships brought goods to them once every two years. The houses became simple for the materials were bleak and the white people worked hard to keep out the Indians and the Eskimo. This helped to feed the wars between the Indians and the Eskimo. Even now there is a division between the two from this event. Finally, the steamship The Labrador was built and could get in and out more easily to the area and Fort Chino became a bustling center for missionaries, drunks, gold miners, prostitutes, and history professors. This was named by the United States Government as the Ungava District and we get funding for our schools today from this grant started around 1866.

"All right, now the creation stories that come in groups, we love to tell stories, each one of us so if one of us gets tired the other can take over!"

The Story
of
Coming of Creation

Man was created from nothing. It was summer and he journeyed until he found a woman living on another land. They joined to become husband and wife. Once they shared the company of the other, they knew that soon death would come to visit them. The Great Spirit Tugaksoak or Great Tung Ak told them in dreams that people having light hair and white skin would come in an immense umiak or carved out tree trunk. Tugaksoak turned the man into a small dog and the woman into a small dog, telling them that they were part of a great magic to come. He set one of the small dogs, for they were about the size of a new puppy, on a chip of wood and set it adrift in the water. The other small dog he placed carefully in an old sealskin boot and placed this boot in the water. The two drifted apart with the different winds pulling them in different directions. Over time, the small dog on the chip returned with Indians from the south. They settled to build up a settlement, developed traditions, language and trade with one another. The other small dog had been completely forgotten until one morning the lookout called out that a glacier was drifting into the bay with a white skinned people who had light hair.

Once the small dog stood on the beach, he turned into a man and called out, "We have come and we have brought new curious goods from far away to share with you. These things will change your lives!" When the man stopped speaking he turned back into a small dog. The other small dog raced down to him. They were united once again after a very long time.

One of the new curious goods was an axe. A man was cutting down a tree when he noticed that the chips continued in motion as they fell from his ax blows. Those chips fell into the water to become water creatures. The chips falling on the land became land animals. Before this the people did not know of hunting for there were no animals to hunt. The water was filled with seaweed which when it came up on the beach turned into berry bushes, trees, shrubs, and grass. The darker richer grasses were gifts from the walrus, but that is another story.

It so happened at about this time there was a woman whose husband died. She was all alone and in need of food and shelter. The woman had a group of strangers to cling to for food and charity. The strangers were not happy with this woman hanging on to them and decided to move to another location. The strangers put all of their goods into an umiak, gathered up the woman to put her in as well and set out into the bay. When they were quite a distance from land, they picked up the woman and threw her overboard. The woman was frantic in the freezing cold waters, she struggled to grab hold of the side of the boat, but they cut off her fingers kicking her away from them. Her fingers when they fell into the water turned into seals and walrus, whales, and white bears. The woman in despair screamed out her revenge on them, she was determined to not let them get away with this horrible deed.

Every since that time the seals and walrus swim quickly away when they see a man, but the whales and white bears remember her words and they attempt to strike back in revenge for what happened to the woman. Many a small vessel has been overturned by a whale and many a man has been attacked by the white bears.

The children of the old ones loved to run and play on a cliff overhanging the sea. The older children would watch the younger children in case they got to close to the edge. Below these noisy children icebergs were floating in the water and the strip of land along the shore was not yet loosened to permit the seals to approach. As the day warmed, a large crack formed in the ice and the seals started to come on the shore. The children were busy running about in the cold wind never thinking to look below for seals. They continued with their games.

The men of the village heard the call of "Seals." They pulled out their kayaks, spears, and pushed into the freezing water. The children not aware of the importance of what was happening below started throwing clumps of mud over the edge of the cliff to frighten the seals. The seals dove into the water disappearing under the floating icebergs. The men saw all this from their kayaks.

One of older men raised his spear into the sky to call out, "I wish the cliff would topple over and bury all those noisy children for scaring the seals." Before his sentence was finished the cliff fell into the freezing water. The children were crushed on the huge rocks and stones at the bottom. Here they were changed into sea pigeons with red feet. To this day you can go there and see the sea pigeons playing on the rocks at the base of the cliff.

This old man was told to leave the area. They told him to hurry and get out, go away and live where people would not bother him and not be bothered by him. This old man had an old elk hide bed blanket and in his hurry to leave he had left it behind. He called this old elk hide bed blanket 'kak.' When he hurried back into the village to get his old elk hide bed blanket the people asked him why he had come back and as he hurried he called out 'kak' and was promptly turned into a raven. Now the people use this word to call the raven.

There was another old man who had no family. He chopped on a tree with his ax and two chips came to life. They had feathers and beaks but no decorations on them. He called them his children and decided to color them. He picked up the bird of the water and painted it with a white breast and square spots on its back. When he saw it he burst out laughing for it was the funniest bird he had ever seen. The Loon was embarrassed and escaped into the water. Now when you see a loon it swims with its white breast showing but keeps its back hidden in the water.

The other bird hurried away from the old man only to fall into a pot of black paint. This didn't stop the bird, the paint dried as he ran, finally to fly away and become the raven. This raven flew over a violent commotion on the beach nearby. A group of women had to walk over a thin area of land in order to get to some sweet berries. The women were in an argument as to when the water would flow over the land mass and how soon they should leave. The tide came in sooner than one woman and her children expected and she was stuck. She went up onto the high cliff and called out to fishermen in a boat. The boat did not turn, the woman became confused and certain that no cared if she was left there with her children.

The children went down to the water. Carefully the older children carried the younger on their backs as they waded through the high tide on the land mass under the water. The mother saw her children leave her. She called to them from high up on the cliff but as she did she changed into a gull who now shouts over and over again, "go over, go over, go over." The gulls still say that when they cry out today.

These small children were exceptionally smart. Now that they had no mother they would play along the edge of a high cliff making toy houses of mud. The other children envied them for their cleverness at making these toy houses with small doors and mud walls. The oldest one was given the name 'Zulugagnak' or 'like a raven.' After a time the people forgot about these small children and they turned into swallows who to this day build small mud houses on the edge of the cliffs.

Another mother who lived on the other side of the bay had so many children she could not feed or clothe them. She was constantly begging for food, searching for food. She worked trying to find a dwelling that would keep the children dry in the rainy season which was all the time. After years of this hard task she was turned into a wolf as were her children. They are still there roaming the hills searching for food, living in the gullies of the runoffs and around the caves of the cliffs.

There was a ghastly spirit who lived up high on the mountain range above the peoples' settlements. He was punished for something terrible he had done to the Creator. This ghastly spirit was not only isolated from all other spirits but he was cursed with lice. They ate at his body all day and all night. Finally the ghastly spirit was so filled with rage that he exploded and his body parts and the lice flew into the air only to land on the settlements below.

This was only the beginning of many troubles. As the settlements grew, more men and woman arrived who were not as hard working as those who set up the villages. A man had a wife who was very pretty, didn't speak often, and was good at dancing but as for her wifely duties she was lazy. It was a custom that when the husband returned from an expedition of the hunt, his wife would take his coat to scrape off the dirt and mud leaving them to hang dry. On one occasion the husband returned home late at night, exhausted from his great expedition. His wife had missed him and was eager to spend time with him and did not scrape the dirt and mud from his coat.

In the morning, the man rose early to go back out. The men of the village were eager to get as much hunting done as possible before the cold winds would race down the valley. He quietly left his wife sleeping on the bed pallet, feeling his way in the dark he grabbed his coat. The dirt and mud clung to his hands. "Oh, no, how filthy, what a wife I have who would rather crawl into bed than be sure her husband's coat is clean!" He flung the dirt and mud particles that were stuck to his hand at his wife as they flew through the air these particles turned into mosquitoes. Ever since that time in the spring, when the women are cleaning the clothes outside from the long winter, the mosquitoes come to bite them reminding them of the lazy wife.

Hunters had a hard time with or without wives. There was a great hunter who lived alone. Each day he would leave at dawn to go out to enjoy his hunt. Some days he brought home food while other days he did not, but he lived alone so he was not worried. After a time he noticed that when he came home his house was dutifully in order. The clothes were cleaned and put on the shelf and the plates were cleanly stacked on the drying board.

This bothered the hunter for he felt someone was entering his house to go through his things. Early one morning, he gathered up his spear, put on his coat, took some fresh bread in a bundle and left the house. This time he hid in the bushes near the house and watched. Birds flew in and out of the open window. A fox loped by to go behind the house. A snake sunned itself on his front step, but no person entered his house. The man grew tired in the afternoon sun. He decided to go inside his home and take a nap, but when he entered the house there stood the most beautiful woman he had ever seen.

"Are you the one who is cleaning my house?" he asked her.

"Yes, your house is a fine house and you were in need of a woman's touch," she replied.

He noticed the woman's clothes were made of a material he had never seen for the material glistened in the light and appeared to almost float around her. When he glanced into the sleeping area he saw a fox skin hanging on a line.

This hunter accepted her as his wife. He would leave early to hunt and she stayed and cleaned, fixed his food, and provided for him in her wifely duties. On one night, however, he wrinkled up his nose and stared at her. She looked at him. "What is wrong?"

"What is that nasty smell? Where is it coming from?" He looked around the room. The woman glared at him and in an instant she was up pulling off her clothing, sliding into the fox skin and before he could understand what was happening she had loped off into the night.

She never returned.

At this time there happened to be an orphan boy who lived with a family that badly abused him. They made him sleep outside by the skinning shed. When they had extra food they would throw it out to him, but they would not allow him to have a knife or come inside the house. When they were angry at each other they would go out back to beat the orphan boy severely. His was a desperately sad life.

The youngest daughter of the nasty people would sneak food out to the orphan. She brought him a knife and on cold nights she gave him a blanket which he hid. The orphan boy dreamt of leaving, he thought only of escaping these horrid people, of getting away from this pain. He made several plans to escape but always something would happen to defeat it.

Finally one night he lay outside and stared up at the moon. As he studied the moon he saw the face of a man staring back down at him. Lifting his hands up to the moon he called up to the man, "Can you help me get out of here?" The man in the moon descended only to come upon the young orphan boy to beat him. The moon hit him over and over again and with each blow the orphan boy grew taller and taller, more and more muscular and had more knowledge gained.

The man from the moon said to the orphan, "It is up to you as to how you lead your life, don't ask others to lead your life for you!" The man flew back up to the moon. The orphan walked along the beach throwing rocks the size of boulders into the bay. He made new islands and found that he could leap up the cliffs with a single step. That night he learned of his strength and abilities.

When the morning sun came up the orphan was at the door of his home. Shoving the door open he confronted the abusive family. The father didn't know who he was for the orphan was tall, strong, and spoke with a loud voice. "You!" called out the orphan as he lifted up the horrid father and ripped his head off. The family ran in all directions to flee from the orphan. The tall orphan slaughtered each of his abusers. The only one left standing was the young daughter. As he reached to take her hand, his body shrank down to that of a normal man. They were married and lived the rest of their lives in comfort.

"Now it is time for us to go or we will miss our plane ride home. Thank you, for the food and the hot chocolate. Look us up if you are ever up north."

Kana'ti and Selu / Cherokee

The tall, straight, white haired man with a very short beard stood on the wooden bridge to the river path in the South Valley. We met there after going to the library. His firm stature, solid square face with piercing dark brown eyes was lifted into the wind. His strong hands waved about as he spoke. His blue denim shirt was ironed, his brown khaki pants creased, and his brown shoes were well polished. "No one remembers the old ones and the testings they went through for us. We are a callous lot. We forget about all of those who went before us. Without them none of us would be here.

"The Nunne'hi were a race of Immortal Spirit People who lived in the highlands of the old Cherokee country. They had a great many townhouses, not like those of today for these they made of wood and housed the whole settlement who had cut the timber. The old townhouses in Pilot Knob were under the old Nikwasi mound in North Carolina. There was another huge townhouse under Blood Mountain at the head of Nottely River in Georgia. These were invisible for the forest surrounded the timber townhouses and hid them well.

"The people there were fond of music and dancing. The drum beat would vibrate down through the forests with such force that the earth would move. They were friendly people and often brought lost wanderers to their townhouses under the mountains and care for them until they were healthy enough to find their way home. They could be tricky though and were known for stealing young women."

An egret flew overhead to land in the irrigated field on our left side. "That bird knows. He knows about his ancestors but we people, we get all involved in the moment and forget about what is important. We bury people and forget them." He jutted his chin to the right where a young boy was cantering down the ditch road on a mule. "All of life is important. When I was a boy this is what the old men told us when we would play close to the river."

The Story
of
Kana'ti and Selu

Long years ago, soon after the world was made, a good hunter and his strong wife lived at Pilot Knob with their only child, a little boy. The father was called Kana'ti (Lucky Hunter) and the strong wife was called Selu (Corn). Regardless of the weather, whenever Kana'ti would go out hunting he always came home with a pack filled with game. Selu would cut up the game, wash it in the river and prepare it in her small kitchen. Their little boy would go down to the river every day to play.

One morning, the old people heard laughing and talking down in the bushes by the river. They thought there were at least two children down there. When the boy came home in the evening his parents asked him who his friend was. "He comes out of the water," said their son, "and he calls himself elder brother. He says his mother threw him into the river where he stays." Selu knew the boy; he had been born from the blood of the game which she washed at the river's edge.

Every day their son would go to play with the river boy and as always, at the end of the day, the water boy would go back into the river. At last one evening Kana'ti said to his son, "Tomorrow, when the other boy comes to play get him to wrestle with you, and when you have your arms around him, hold onto him and call for us." Their son promised to do this.

The next day, the two boys got into a wrestling match. All at once the son began screaming for his father. The parents came at once to see the Wild Boy and the son held him firmly. The Wild Boy called out, "Let me go! You threw me away! Let me go!" But the parents seized the Wild Boy and took him home. They kept him in the house. They tried to tame him. They tried to tame him over and over again. They tried to tame him, but it did not work, he was wild. Finally, the parents realized that the Wild Boy had magic powers and they called him I'nage'utasun'hi (He who grew up in the wild).

The two brothers were constantly getting into trouble for the older boy would lead the younger son into mischief. It was on one occasion that Wild Boy decided to follow Kana'ti to find where he gets all of his game. Each day, the two boys would creep to follow Kana'ti. A few days after they started this, Kana'ti took a bow and some arrows in his hand and started toward the west. The boys waited a little while and then followed him, keeping out of sight until they saw him go into a swamp where there were many small reeds that the hunters used to make arrow shafts. They watched Kana'ti pull up the reeds and place them on his arrows. The Wild Boy decided to turn himself into cotton down to float on Kana'ti's shoulder. Kana'ti knew nothing of this for after he fixed his arrows, he walked up the hill to lift a large rock. No sooner had he lifted the rock, than a buck ran up and out of the hole. Quickly Kana'ti dropped the rock. He shot the buck, pulled his arrow out of the buck, and started back for home.

The Wild Boy returned to his little brother and told him what he had seen. They both agreed to hurry home, say nothing, and return the next day to lift the rock. Kana'ti got home later for he had to carry the heavy buck. The family had a good dinner and in the early morning the two boys set off for the swamp. They took the reeds and placed them on their arrows. They found the rock and with the two of them lifting it, got it up and rolled it to the side. The deer came running out and just as they drew to shoot, another jumped out and then another. The deer were coming so quickly, they became confused.

Wild Boy shot his first arrow, but he hit the deer in the tail. Now the deer's tails are short and go straight up in the air. The son stood and stared. As the deer finished coming up and out, droves of raccoons, rabbits, and all the other four-footed animals, all but the bear because there was no bear then, came out from the hole. Lastly, out flew great flocks that made so much noise with their wings that Kana'ti, who was sitting at home, heard the sound like thunder on the mountains and he knew, "My bad boys are in trouble. I must go and see what they are doing."

Kana'ti hurried up the mountain, becoming more and more worried as the location and the sound was familiar to him. He found the two boys standing by the rock with all of the animals and birds gone. Kana'ti was furious, but he didn't say a word. He went down into the hole and there in the corner were four jars. He kicked the covers off of the jars. Bedbugs, fleas, lice and gnats flew up and out to attack the two boys. They screamed in frightful pain and tried to beat off the insects, but thousands of them were crawling over boys, biting, stinging, and burrowing under their skin. The boys dropped down nearly dead.

Kana'ti stood looking at them until he felt they had had enough. In one motion he knocked the boys with his powerful hand - the insects fell off to fly or crawl away from them. "Now, you will have to learn to hunt or go hungry. I have always provided food for you, but no more. It is time for you to learn the art of the hunt. Go home to your mother. I will try and find us some deer for dinner. Go home!"

The boys got home, but there was no food. Selu told them not to worry, she would go find food. Selu took her basket and started out to the store house. This store house was built upon poles high up from the ground to keep it out of reach of animals. There was a ladder to climb and one door, but there were no other openings. The boys stood and watched her. The Wild Boy said, "Did you notice that everyday Selu goes up to the store house to bring down beans and corn. How does she find corn and beans up there? In the air?"

The store house had always been off limits to the two boys, but now they were curious. When Selu went up the ladder to the store house, the two boys followed quietly behind her. They ran around and climbed up to the back of the store house. They pulled out a piece of clay from between the logs to peek inside the room to watch Selu. She was standing over the basket, in the middle of the room. She leaned over rubbing her stomach, like so, and the basket filled up half full with corn. Selu lifted up her simple shift dress and began rubbing her arm pits, like so, and the other half of the basket filled with beans.

The boys looked at each other. "Our mother is a witch! If we eat any of her corn or beans it will probably kill us!" The Wild Boy shook his head. "We must kill her."

Selu carried the basket down the ladder to wait for the boys. She had read their thoughts. "So, you two boys are going to kill me?"

"Yes," said the boys. "You are a witch!"

"Well," said their mother, "be sure to clear a large piece of ground in front of the house before you do this so you can drag my body seven times around the ground in a circle. Then you must stay up all night and watch to be sure the morning sun touches the ground right after the dew falls. If you do this you will always have corn and beans to eat."

The boys set off at once to clear the ground. Selu watched them and gave her approval. Then they cut off her head to put it up on the store house roof so she could look for her husband. Her body was dragged around the seven circles with her blood flowing corn, but they did not drag her body seven times around the circle that is why corn grows in some places but not in others and why beans only grow when there is just the right amount of sun and dew.

The sun rose after the dew, for the boys had kept each other awake all night to see. The ears of corn were fat and ripe and the beans were ready for picking by the time their father arrived home. Kana'ti was exhausted, for he had searched all night for a deer, but had found none. He asked the boys where their mother was. The boys said, "She was a witch and we killed her. Look up, there is her head by the store house."

Kana'ti stared in disbelief. "I won't stay with you any longer. I am going to the Wolf People." Kana'ti turned and ran to the west, but before he went very far Wild Boy turned himself into a tuft of down to land on his shoulder.

When Kana'ti arrived at the settlement of the Wolf People, they were holding a council in the townhouse. He went in and sat down with the tuft of down on his shoulder. When the Wolf Chief asked Kana'ti his business, he said, "I have two bad boys at home. I want you to go seven days from now and play ball against them." This was code to the Wolf People for them to go in seven days and kill the two boys.

The tuft of down flew into the smoke, up the smoke hole, and out into the air. The Wild Boy took his rightful shape and ran home to his brother. Kana'ti did not return home, but continued walking to the west. The boys began to get ready for the Wolf People. Wild Boy told his brother what to do. They ran around the house in a wide circle until they made a trail all around it excepting on the side where the Wolf People would come, there they left a small open space.

They made four large bundles of arrows and placed them at four different points on the outside of the circle. Then they hid in the woods and waited for the Wolf People. In a day or two a whole party of wolves came and surrounded the house ready for the kill. The wolves did not notice the trail around the house, because they came in where the boys had left the opening, but the moment they went inside the circle the trail changed to a high brush fence and trapped them inside.

The boys on the outside ran around with their arrows and bows and shot them down. The wolves could not jump over the fence most of them were killed. Some escaped through an opening in the brush to get through a swamp close by. The boys ran around the swamp and a circle of fire sprang up in their tracks and set fire to the grass and bushes and burned up nearly all the other Wolves. Only two or three got away and from these have come all the wolves that are now in the world.

There was a village not too far away, the people there heard about what happened to the brothers and the wonderful grain they grew and they wanted some to make their bread. These villagers spread the news about the corn meal with which to make bread and soon strangers were coming from all over to buy the corn meal. The boys were giving away seven grains of corn, giving them directions on how to plant, harvest, and dry the ears to prepare crops for the following years. The most important fact, the boys told the strangers, was to plant the corn the next night on their way home, to watch it all night long, and to do this for every night they travelled. Once they got home they were to plant the corn in the darkness, watch it all night, and the morning there would be enough corn to supply the whole village.

Most of the people by the sixth or seventh night were so tired that they fell asleep. That is why now it takes all summer for the corn to ripen and be ready for harvest in the fall. The corn must be watched and tended through half the year, which before would grow and ripen in one night.

Kana'ti did not return to the boys' home. They missed their father and decided it was time for them to go and find him. The Wild Boy took a gaming wheel and rolled it out on the Darkening Land. It came rolling back to him and showed them that their father was not there. Wild Boy rolled the gaming wheel to the South Land and to the North Land, and each time it told them that their father was not there. Finally, Wild Boy rolled the gaming wheel to the Sun Land in the east, the wheel did not return, telling him that was the land where their father was staying. "Our father is there," pointed Wild Boy, "it is time for us to find him."

The two brothers set off to the east and after several days came upon

Kana'ti walking beside a dog. "You are bad sons," said their father. "Why have you come here?"

The two brothers stepped up their pace to walk beside their father. "Yes, we may be bad, but we always finish what we accomplish to do. We are men now."

Kana'ti pointed to the dog. "This dog over took me four days ago and now you are here, this dog must have something to do with the both of you."

Wild Boy shrugged. "We sent out the gaming wheel and it did not return. That must be the shape it chose to find you."

"Well," Kana'ti said, "you have found me. I will take the lead."

Soon they came to a swamp and Kana'ti told the boys to be quiet and careful, "Something dangerous lives in this swamp, it is best if we get around it quickly and move on silently."

The two boys watched their father move ahead of them. Wild Boy grabbed his brother's arm and said, "Let him go ahead, I want to see what is in the swamp." As soon as Kana'ti was out of sight, the two boys jumped into the swamp.

In the middle of the swamp they found a large panther sleeping. Wild Boy got out an arrow and shot the panther in the side of the head. The panther turned his head and the other brother shot him on that side. The panther turned his head again and the two brothers shot again—thwap, thwap, thwap, thwap. The panther was not hurt by the arrows, he ignored the brothers. Wild Boy nudged his brother and said, "Let's get out of here for there is great magic here that I don't understand."

The two boys caught up with their father, who was waiting for them. Kana'ti called out to them, "Did you find it?"

"Yes," said the boys. "But it never hurt us, we are men!"

Kana'ti was surprised, but said nothing, and they walked on down the path.

After a while Kana'ti turned to them. "Now you must be careful for there are cannibals here called A'nada'duntaski (Roasters). If these guys catch you they will put you in a pot, boil you up, and eat you."

Kana'ti walked ahead. The boys walked slowly behind him, looking to the left and the right. Wild Boy stopped to point at a tree that had been hit by lightning. Wild Boy told his brother to gather some of the splinters from the tree and told him what to do with these splinters if they were to get caught. Little brother did this.

In a while they came to a settlement filled with cannibals. The cannibals raced out, shouting, "Strangers are here, now it is time for a grand feast!" They caught the boys, dragged them into the townhouse, and sent word up and down the settlement to come to a feast that night. The cannibals made up a great fire, put water into a large pot, and set it to boiling, and then seized the Wild Boy and put him in the pot. The little brother was not afraid at all and made no attempt to escape for he just quietly knelt down and put the splinters into the fire, as if to make it burn hotter.

When the cannibals thought the boys should be cooked, they lifted the pot from the fire and in that instant a binding light filled their townhouse, lightning began to dart from one side to the other, striking each cannibal with lightning until not one of the cannibals was left alive. Then the lightning went up through the smoke hole. In the next moment the two boys were standing outside the townhouse as if nothing had happened.

They ran ahead and soon caught up with Kana'ti. He turned in shock. "What? What are you two doing here?"

"We are men, we never give up, and we are great men!" the boys said together.

"Did the cannibals let you go? I heard they had captured you and were planning a feast tonight to eat you both?"

Wild Boy shook his head. "They brought us into their townhouse, but they never hurt us." Kana'ti said nothing for he just went on down the path with his dog. The brothers followed him. The three of them with the dog walked and walked to the place where the sun comes out. The sky was just coming down when they arrived there. They waited until it went up again to go through to the other side. Kana'ti moved quickly ahead of them, for the brothers kept challenging everything they met along the way.

When they finally got to the place of the other side, they found Kana'ti and Selu sitting together. Their parents received them kindly and told them they could stay there, but then the two brothers were to go and live where the sun goes down. That was the place for the two brothers - the place where the sun goes down!

The boys stayed with their parents seven days and then they gathered up food and supplies to go the Darkening Land, where they are now. We call the two of them Anisga'ya Tsunsdi (Little Men), and when they talk to each other, we hear low rolling thunder in the west.

Now we say:

Go to the top of the mountain.

Drop your stone on the pile for the Spirits.

Go to the top of the mountain.

Drop your juniper on the pile for the Spirits.

Your life will be a safe journey.

CPSIA information can be obtained
at www.ICGtesting.com
Printed in the USA
LVHW102145280622
722351LV00021B/576

9 780865 348332